Despite all the confident, boisterous pronounce[...]
are dying or dead, liturgical worship—anchor[...]
by historic hymns, and centered on the Eucharist—quietly r[...]
In this personal, journalistic look at some of the young adults finding their
way back to it, Winfield Bevins helps explain liturgy's beguiling persistence.
This book chronicles a remarkably hopeful trend in today's churches.

Wesley Hill, assistant professor of biblical
studies, Trinity School for Ministry

There is a hunger among this generation to recover the historic roots of
the Christian faith for discipleship and mission. Winfield Bevins' new
book offers a clear and compelling account of why young adults across
North America are embracing liturgy. If you want to learn more about this
movement and why it matters, this book is for you.

Alan Hirsch, author of *The Forgotten Ways*

Winfield Bevins is an expert on the mission and renewal of the church, and
with the research for this book, he is now well versed in the attitudes and
practices of young people regarding liturgy and sacrament. *Ever Ancient,
Ever New* brings together the best of Winfield, yielding something like
a field guide to the mix of Gospel, culture, church, young people and
liturgy. This is a must-read if you are trying to reach and disciple young
people in liturgical forms.

Bishop Todd Hunter, author of *Giving Church Another Chance*

Younger Christians are being spiritually renewed today through ancient
Christian worship, community, and spiritual practice. Weaving wide-
ranging research with scholarly wisdom, Winfield Bevins tells us their
stories, and we find ourselves renewed as well.

Joel Scandrett, director of the Robert E. Webber
Center, Trinity School for Ministry

Young people sometimes discover that worship that aims to be timely can
grow stale. Instead, they seek worship that is timeless. In *Ever Ancient,
Ever New,* Winfield Bevins introduces us to the wide array of choices they
have discovered in that search.

Frederica Mathewes-Green, author of
Welcome to the Orthodox Church

If you want to know why so many young people in the United States are embracing liturgy, you must read Winfield Bevins' new book!

Lyle W. Dorsett, editor of *The Essential C. S. Lewis*

In the swirling currents of opinions and the changing tides of trends, the church is in need of an anchor and a compass. Winfield Bevins uncovers the heart of historic Christian worship in order to steady us and to guide us. He helps us see that the rise of ancient practices in the church today is not a kind of nostalgia, but rather a response to our amnesia: we have forgotten the gospel-shaped, Christ-centered truth found in the logic and language of the liturgy. This book will beckon you not so much to a return but to a renewal, and I welcome it.

Glenn Packiam, associate senior pastor,
New Life Church and author, *Blessed Broken Given* and *Discover the Mystery of Faith*

Winfield celebrates the wonder, beauty, and richness of liturgy. He is a wise and joyful tour guide and storyteller of the movement among Christians who are returning to historic, creedal, and liturgical reflections of Christianity. The ancient roots of the Christian faith empower spiritual formation and mission. Because Winfield cares deeply about church planting, he not only writes about how liturgy affects worshippers regarding their personal spiritual vitality but also how it shapes churches and Christians for missionary zeal for the world.

Justin S. Holcomb, Episcopal priest,
author, and seminary professor

Bevins has done such a good thing with this book. It is a scholarly accounting of a crucial phenomenon in the present age while, at the same time, a guide to people caught up in this phenomenon. Bevins describes the modern return to ancient practices with a light touch and a generous, fearless love of orthodoxy. He tells many stories in this book, gathered over many years and multiple cultures. I found parts of my story in almost all of them, and I suspect you will, too.

Stephen Backhouse, author of *Kierkegaard: A Single Life*

EVER ANCIENT, EVER NEW

ALSO BY WINFIELD BEVINS

*Marks of a Movement: What the Church
Today Can Learn from the Wesleyan Revival*

*Grow at Home: A Beginner's
Guide to Family Discipleship*

*Our Common Prayer: A Field Guide
to the Book of Common Prayer*

*Creed: Connect to the Basic Essentials
of Historic Christian Faith*

EVER ANCIENT,
EVER NEW

The Allure of Liturgy for a New Generation

WINFIELD BEVINS

ZONDERVAN

Ever Ancient, Ever New
Copyright © 2019 by Winfield Bevins

ISBN 978-0-310-56613-7 (softcover)

ISBN 978-0-310-10718-7 (audio)

ISBN 978-0-310-56614-4 (ebook)

Requests for information should be addressed to:
Zondervan, *3900 Sparks Dr. SE, Grand Rapids, Michigan 49546*

Art direction: Tammy Johnson
Cover design: Darren Welch
Cover photography: Lightstock
Interior design: Kait Lamphere

Printed in the United States of America

19 20 21 22 23 24 25 26 27 28 /LSC/ 15 14 13 12 11 10 9 8 7 6 5 4 3 2 1

For Ross Jenkins,
With deep appreciation and gratitude.
This book would not have been possible without you.

CONTENTS

FOREWORD

There used to be two kinds of churches. Historic churches connected to historic denominations, like The Episcopal Church, the Presbyterian Church (USA), the Methodist Church, the Roman Catholic Church, and the various national branches of The Orthodox Church, and churches that were not quite as historic, often called free churches or non-denominational churches, like The American Baptist Churches or the Southern Baptist Church. The former have constraints imposed by the denomination's historic teaching, practices, and leaders; the latter are autonomous and can do mostly what they think the Lord would have them do. Change for the former is a challenge; change for the latter is much easier, though one cannot pretend it's as easy as that.

Now there are three kinds. Historic churches, autonomous churches, and autonomous churches picking up what the historic churches have always done and sometimes leaving the world of autonomy for the wisdom of a denomination. At the center of this movement, and Winfield Bevins' research proves that this is no fly-by-night experiment by a few creative or restoratives and that this is a genuine, growing movement, is the lectionary and liturgy. That is, churches that at one time were part of a movement to get away from all things formal and institutional are now seeing the wisdom of the formal use of the lectionary and the potency of liturgy.

While some have abandoned the autonomous world of free churches to join the Roman Catholic Church or the Orthodox Church, a far larger number is shifting toward The Anglican Communion. At the heart of this shift is nothing less than the beauty and theological grandeur of *The Book of Common Prayer*, whose words—Alan Jacobs tells us—are "to be living words in the mouths of those who have a living faith."[1] Which has been the knock on all lectionary and liturgy driven churches. That is, routine, rote, rut-sunk recitations of ancient words can deaden and have deadened many, and many in the free church traditions continue to make that claim.

I am not one, and neither is Winfield. I grew up in an autonomous church loosely connected to the Conservative Baptists, and I had no reason to break loose and join the Presbyterians or the Methodists of the Episcopals in my home town. When Kris and I and our two children, Laura and Lukas, moved to Nottingham, England, we were invited to attend St Peter's Church (Toton) with a curate named John Corrie. We had never used *The Book of Common Prayer*, but on the very first Sunday, along with wondering why the music didn't have notes and worrying about when to stand or sit, I heard for the first time the words of the collects, those weekly prayers recited, often from rote memory. My born-again past met the living faith of living words in the collects, and I was overwhelmed. And have been ever since.

I am an Anglican Deacon today, Canon Theologian to Bishop Todd Hunter in the C4SO diocese, which is one group in The Anglican Church of North America (a denomination with a historic past), and I am so largely because the worship ordered by *The Book of Common Prayer* affirms in me what I most believe about what Sunday worship and daily prayer ought to be: sacred words for sacred moments for a sacred people gathered for a sacred purpose. This ordered worship in *The Book of Common Prayer* is not magical, and without faith, the words deaden.

What I have witnessed in the last few decades, and one cannot minimize the impact of John Stott, J. I. Packer, Robert Webber, and the scores of Wheaton students who became Anglican and have become leaders in the American evangelical scene, is that when a genuine born-again faith meets up with *The Book of Common Prayer*, the encounter is transforming. The movement sketched by Winfield Bevins tells the story of many who know that all creativity is more boring than all tradition, that the words of the lectionary and liturgy are theologically sound and gospel-saturated, and that one suddenly comes into fresh weekly and daily contact with the great tradition of the church.

Winfield is right: this way is "ever ancient" and at the same time "ever new."

Scot McKnight,
Professor of New Testament,
Northern Seminary

INTRODUCTION

Late have I loved You, O Beauty
ever ancient, ever new!
ST. AUGUSTINE

S arah Grace is a twenty-year-old university student who has a contagious smile and a deep love for God. During a recent trip to England, she had an unusual life-changing encounter. Sarah and a group of twenty other university students traveled to London to sing as a part of a choral cathedral residency. During the trip, she had her first encounter with traditional liturgy. Through this encounter, Sarah found that embracing the church's ancient roots transformed her faith and widened her perspective of worship in ways she had never imagined.

The experience was intimidating and somewhat unexpected. "Singing hymns and processing through the congregation—sitting and standing at designated times—and reading corporate prayers didn't exactly fall within my realm of comfort," she said. "However, once I began to focus on *what* was being said or sung, rather than *the way* it was done, the services took on a whole new meaning." Through this experience, Sarah became open to some of the historic, liturgical practices of worship. "Suddenly," she said, "the words of believers from thousands of years before were on my lips, ringing out as true and pure as the day they were written. I was connecting with the universal church in ways that transcended time and space, and I was deepening roots that I didn't even realize I had. Every element of the service, from the breathtaking architecture to the ethereal choral melodies to the heartfelt recitation of the liturgy, presented me with an opportunity to bask in the transcendence of God and to respond with awestruck praise."

When I first heard Sarah Grace describe her encounter, I thought to myself, *I've heard this story before. I've lived this story!* As someone who has made the journey from non-liturgical churches to helping lead churches that regularly practice liturgical worship, Sarah's statements about the allure of liturgy ring true for me as well.

I was raised in a Southern Baptist home, but I came to faith in a Pentecostal church. I gleaned a great deal from these traditions and the experiences they offered, experiences that continue to shape me today. I experienced being "born again" and "filled with the Spirit." Yet despite the many positive contributions these traditions made to my spiritual journey, it felt as if something was missing, but I couldn't discern what that something was. Reflecting back on my early years as a believer, I now realize I longed for a sense of connection to the past, to the traditions, practices, and beliefs that have shaped Christian experience for the past two thousand years. This longing wasn't a rejection of my heritage but has taken shape as a desire to be part of a more sacramental tradition, one connected to the historic Christian faith.

I come from a "low church" background, from a church that believed in the power of the Bible but had little interest in a more structured worship service. We did not speak of liturgy, and even if we had one, it was not intentionally connected to the past, to the historic church. I always felt like something was missing. I longed for a deeper, broader expression of my faith. I needed more than repeated admonitions to pray and read the Bible by myself. Time and time again, I found I couldn't go deeper on my own; I was searching for something to guide me into the depths of God's love and grace. I didn't know it at the time, but I needed what liturgy had to offer.

In seminary, I worked at a church that faithfully preached the Word every week but only celebrated Communion once a year. And even when we celebrated the Lord's Supper, the church did not approach the practice as a sacrament. Communion was a memorial exercise—a vague remembrance of Christ's sacrifice. To be honest, it felt like Communion was simply a last-minute add-on to the service with little, if any, spiritual significance. I knew this practice had held deep significance for generations of believers, and I sensed that there had to be more to celebrating it than I was currently experiencing.

One day I stumbled into a local Episcopal church. As I entered the service, I wasn't sure what I would encounter. Sitting in the pew, I fumbled my way through the liturgy—the established order of worship—with the help of the rector and three elderly ladies. To my surprise, I encountered the risen Christ at the Lord's Table that day in a way I had never experienced before. What was different? I found that the liturgy enabled me to *experience* Christ, not just in my head and heart, but also through my bodily senses. I felt a palpable sense of the sacred in that worship service, a connection with something transcendent and other-worldly. This particular Episcopal church had created a sacred space through its beautiful aesthetic of historic architecture, the reading of Scripture, and the recitation of several historic prayers. I felt the burning sensation of the wine down my throat as I sipped the fruit of the vine from a chalice.

In that little parish church, I fell in love with the beauty and mystery of liturgy. Even though much of the service was foreign to me, it felt strangely like I had come home. Much like Sarah Grace, I was looking for a connection to my larger Christian family, and the attraction of liturgy was that it offered me a window into practices and patterns that have shaped Christians for generations. The roots of the Christian church began not with modern evangelicalism but at the time of Christ, long before the modern Western church. I longed to see, experience, and understand liturgical practices and how they were connected to those historic roots. Like many contemporary

Christians, I had neglected two thousand years of church history. I was beginning to realize there is much we can glean from the past as we seek to develop Christian practices for this generation. For years I had felt like a spiritual orphan, unaware of my rich family heritage. Like a fatherless child discovering a rich family genealogy for the first time, I came to understand my own spiritual genealogy through the ancient practices of the liturgy.

Over the past decade, I've learned that I'm not alone in my experience. I've spent countless hours speaking with young adults who have shared similar stories of deep curiosity and interest in the historic expressions of the Christian faith and the practices of the liturgy. This is one reason I've written this book: to learn why young adults who are natives to the digital world and heavily reliant upon technology are so interested in traditions that have been around for two thousand years. I know what first led *me* to follow these longings, but I wanted to know more. *What is the allure of liturgy for a new generation?*

As I've interviewed pastors and talked with young adults around the United States, I've discovered a generation that is searching for God in the midst of unprecedented social and cultural change. These are sincere Christ-followers looking to face the challenges of a postmodern, post-Christian world that is increasingly multicultural, secularized, and globalized. The result of my journey is this book, a profile of a slice of this emerging generation that is seeking to rediscover the ancient roots of the Christian faith.

For many years now, articles, surveys, and news reports have lamented the steady flow of young people leaving the church in North America at an alarming rate.[1] Yet while a growing number of young adults are leaving the church, there are other trends as well. Some younger Christians are choosing to remain in the fold of Christianity, but that doesn't mean they are content with the existing expressions of evangelical faith. Many young believers, from different backgrounds and traditions, are staying in the church while embracing a liturgical expression of the faith. And while it is most noticeable among young adults, this trend is true of people of various ages and backgrounds as well, believers who are seeking to recover ancient practices of the Christian faith. This growing phenomenon has found expression at universities, colleges, and seminary campuses. I've spent several years speaking to many of these individuals, interviewing them and asking them why they are turning to the past and how they are integrating it into their own faith. I have come to realize it is just the latest expression of a continual trend in every generation as believers seek to recover the historic roots of the church. Commenting on the movement we see today, author and Anglican Bishop Todd Hunter proclaims, "There is something in the air today, something in the spirit of our age, something in the Spirit that is leading thousands, maybe millions, of people to reconsider liturgical forms of worship."[2]

Perhaps the most notable scholar to recognize this growing trend among Christians was the late theologian Robert Webber. During his lifetime, Webber wrote more than forty books, including the fascinating story of his own journey, *Evangelicals on the Canterbury Trail*, first published in 1985. In this book Webber expounds upon his own personal progression from being a member of a fundamentalist Baptist church to becoming a professor at Wheaton College and eventually joining the Episcopal Church. After experiencing this shift in his own life, Webber realized that many younger Christians during his own lifetime had embarked on similar journeys toward recovering the church's ancient rhythms of liturgy. As an attempt at explaining this shift, Webber analyzed the movement and found that "the primary source for younger evangelical spirituality, other than the Bible, is the past."[3] Driven by a deeply felt need for belonging, these individuals were denying modernity's valuation of newness and reaching toward a tradition that runs much deeper than their own lifetime. Today, almost forty years since Webber published his story, we see this trend continuing with a new generation of young believers.

While Webber's research and writing favored evangelically friendly liturgical streams, the movement is not confined to evangelicals alone. Webber's voice was joined by author Phyllis Tickle, who believed that the trend of reaching back to the past is taking place among the next generation. Tickle believed that it is not evangelicals who are on the Canterbury trail, "rather, it is a much larger company . . . who, in large part, are either on the Canterbury trail or are absorbing and re-employing the characteristics, spirituality, and practices of pilgrims."[4] Many of these "pilgrims" she describes are young adults. After encountering such power in traditional practices and liturgy, they have begun to seek places that effectively incorporate ancient practices into modern contexts.

Throughout this book, I want to share how my own encounters have led me to explore the allure of liturgy for those in a new generation. For the past two years, I have traveled across the United States, Canada, and England visiting churches, cathedrals, universities, and seminaries. I have listened to dozens of young adults share how they have embraced Christian liturgy. I have heard stories about how liturgy is impacting many lives, and I have interviewed hundreds of young adults and leaders to hear their stories about how liturgy has impacted their faith. They are hipsters, authors, teachers, students, pastors, musicians, and people from all walks of life, but they have one thing in common: they have found a home in the liturgical practices of the historic church.

You may notice that I often use the term "young adults." I'm intentionally using this phrase because the trends I've observed aren't limited to a single generation. By "young adults" I'm roughly speaking of those born from the early 1970s through the mid-1990s, a span that includes millennials and the younger members of Generation X (or "Gen X" for short). I live with one foot on each side of this "new generation" I speak about, as a Gen Xer married to a millennial. In addition, I live, work, and teach in college and seminary communities, so much of my life involves interacting with the "young adults" of today.

I've divided *Ever Ancient, Ever New* into three parts to help you better navigate the contents: foundations, journeys, and practices. Part 1 lays the foundations of why young adults are drawn to liturgy. Part 2 examines various paths that are leading them into embracing liturgy. And Part 3 looks at how liturgy offers practices that can be lived out in our daily lives and how those practices prepare us to live out our faith in the world.

In the following pages, we will explore how a new generation is finding new depths to their faith as they rediscover liturgy. We will see how and why liturgy has beckoned them deeper, what types of churches and communities foster this convergence of old and new, and much more. My hope is that in reading this book and their stories in it, you will be better able to recognize and appreciate how ancient practices and principles can help you grow in Christ with a holistic and embodied faith. As we walk alongside several young people who are traveling this journey, we'll see firsthand how traditional liturgical and ancient practices are providing fresh expressions of a timeless faith in the ever-changing context of postmodernity.

We won't find the answers to our current church crisis by inventing new, innovative ideas, nor will an awareness of the past magically fix the problems of the present. Instead, we'll find signposts pointing toward the future as we explore the intersection where the past and the present meet. The young adults in this book embody this place of *convergence*, and together, we could very well be on the verge of a new wave of God's grace as we discover the great foundations of faith and look toward the future.

Finally, I don't think the recovery of liturgy is merely a trend among young people; it is something much bigger than I first realized. What I've come to recognize is that there appears to be something significant undergirding the recovery of liturgy. Perhaps you have asked the question, "What about liturgy is attracting young people, and why does it matter for today?" I have come to the conclusion that liturgy, when rightly appropriated, is one of the best ways for us to make disciples in a postmodern context. It is this emphasis—the appropriation of ancient practices for disciple formation today—that is the unifying theme of this book.

My hope in exploring the profound vitality of the ancient practices these young adults have discovered is that regardless of your age or background, your faith will be renewed as you hear their stories and encounter the power of liturgical practices for yourself. I hope that through this book, you will find fresh ways of exploring and engaging with these historic practices in meaningful ways. To help you do this, I have added reflection questions and practices at the end of each chapter. Let's get started!

PART 1

FOUNDATIONS

CHAPTER 1

THE NEW SEARCH FOR LITURGY

I still haven't found what I'm looking for.

U2

Everyone loves a good story. Story relates truth by painting a world and then drawing the reader into its landscape. There is something captivating about a good story, and all the truly good stories echo the One Great Story, the Bible's story of God's redemptive plan for humankind throughout the ages. God is *the* great storyteller, and history is one grand narrative of God's redemptive love for lost humanity.

Think about the books and movies you've enjoyed and loved. How have they influenced your desires and thoughts? It's likely they presented the narrative in a way that invited you, the reader or viewer, to inhabit the story. Think of John Bunyan's *Pilgrim's Progress* or J.R.R. Tolkien's Lord of the Rings series. Stories like these remind us that a good story does more than convey information, it forms a relationship with the reader. As we journey through this book together, I've included stories and quotes from people who have been formed by the historic practices and liturgy of the Christian church. My hope is that their stories will resonate with your own journey as a follower of Christ in a way that reveals the allure of liturgy for every generation. So as we begin this first chapter, I want to begin with a question: What does it mean to rediscover the wonder and beauty of liturgy?

Let's begin with a few stories from some of the young adults I've met.

STORIES OF EXPERIENCE AND OF CHANGE

Rick is twenty-seven years old. He was raised in a conservative evangelical church, and he learned to sing traditional hymns and memorized dozens of Bible verses as a child. He spent much of his youth at church, always there "whenever the doors were open." As he grew older, Rick began to feel that his church was too rigid, that it might be hindering him from experiencing the fullness of the Christian life. He looked for answers in the verses he had memorized, quoting them to himself, hoping these isolated verses would give him the fullness of life he wanted. Eventually Rick grew weary and left his childhood tradition to explore a more charismatic church for several years. There he encountered the gifts of the Spirit and began to thrive—until the newness of the experience wore off. Even after these experiences, at the end of the day Rick felt that something was still missing. He couldn't articulate what that missing piece was; he simply felt incomplete. Having been raised with a solid doctrinal foundation, he had developed a keen respect for the Scriptures and he'd had vibrant spiritual experiences, but he still felt that there had to be something more. In a last attempt to find what was missing (and at the risk of alienating himself from his evangelical background), Rick began attending a Roman Catholic church. Unexpectedly, he found himself at home in the liturgically infused services. He'd always heard from others how boring and dry "those Catholic services" were, but when he experienced them for himself, he found he was overcome by the beauty of the ancient forms and rhythms. It was foreign, yet oddly, it felt like what he'd been searching for.

Rick began attending the church regularly and realized he had found his home in the Catholic tradition.

Jennifer was raised in a liberal Methodist church where she was taught the importance of social justice, sacrificial service, and helping the less fortunate. Her upbringing focused less on the gospel or the teachings of the Bible and instead emphasized the outworking of its social implications. Like Rick, Jennifer began to feel that something was missing in her faith. Looking for a spiritual experience outside of her comfort zone, Jennifer attended a Pentecostal congregation where she experienced a powerful "baptism of the Spirit." When this happened, her faith became something personal, coming alive in a way it never had before. However, after a few years in this church, she left in search of something more. Today, Jennifer attends a rural Episcopal church, where she was recently confirmed as a member.

The journeys of Jennifer and Rick began on different ends of the spectrum, yet they end in similar places. I see their spiritual journeys as more than a coincidence. As I've observed in interviews with people from a variety of backgrounds across the country, Jennifer's and Rick's stories represent a larger movement of young adults who are looking to fill a void in their faith journey. Their search has led them to explore different streams of Christianity, and many of them have found their home in more liturgical expressions of the Christian faith.

But what lies behind this movement? Why are young people from different ecclesial backgrounds embracing liturgical streams of the faith? I began exploring this question by focusing on another question: What did these young adults feel they were *missing* in the church backgrounds in which they were raised?

THE SOURCE OF CULTURAL SHIFT

To understand why individuals are engaging this journey toward liturgy, we must begin by looking at the cultural shifts happening in

North America. Many of postmodernity's ideals play an important role in how people think about their faith and what they feel is "missing" from their existing tradition.[1] In many ways, the churches these young adults have abandoned represent holdovers from the modern era, locked in a way of being and doing church that no longer speaks to the felt needs of a new generation. Derived from the Latin root meaning "now," "modernity" refers to a historical and social period that focused on individualism and human freedom, and which emphasized social, scientific, and technological progress. The Age of Modernity can be nicely summed up by the words of René Descartes, the father of modern reason: "I think, therefore I am."

Though the outworking of cultural shifts took centuries to unfold, the effects of modernity were catastrophic for the church. The rise of modernity was accompanied by a rejection of historical religious values and religious life in favor of the newest ideas, philosophies that elevated the human mind as the supreme source of knowledge. If a person couldn't prove an idea through the empirical scientific method, then it was no longer considered true knowledge. An emphasis on reason, logic, and the materialist worldview of scientism led to a denial of the supernatural nature of Christianity. Many people began to doubt the history of Christianity because not everything taught in the Bible could be proven scientifically.

The modern era also helped give rise to the Industrial Revolution, which valued progress, efficiency, and pragmatism. In all of this, the church was profoundly influenced by the values of the culture, and Christianity began to lose its emphasis on holistic spirituality, embracing pragmatism and progress. As a result, our culture began to focus on the present rather than looking to the past for wisdom and continuity.

Churches in North America began to define success by measuring growth, emphasizing size and numbers over traditional signs of spiritual fruitfulness and biblical holiness. In the 1990s, many churches embraced business and marketing strategies to help them grow larger. They developed slick, well-executed programming to boost attendance, and in an effort to reach young people, churches turned their youth rooms into concert halls. They used games, gimmicks, and gadgets in order to be relevant and cool in hopes of attracting youth. Commenting on this trend, Jason Brian Santos says, "Many of our larger churches have become mini-malls, hosting coffee shops, bookstores and hair salons."[2] But were they successful? The end result of attempts to "woo" the world with the world's ways has produced a generation of *consumers*—individuals who sit in the driver's seat and dictate what and how the church should meet their needs—rather than radically *committed disciples* of Jesus Christ. The product of centuries of individualism combined with a turn toward the successful pragmatism of American business practices, consumer Christianity sees the church as a place of goods and services rather than a place of growth, service, giving, and going back into the world through mission.

Many young people today are not interested in a church that provides a slightly different version of what the world can give them. If the church is just another vendor of services—not even a good one in some cases—what does it have that they cannot get elsewhere?

Young adults are rejecting the modern church in growing numbers, and one reason is that they have grown up in a transitional society and have a different worldview from Christians of previous generations. The church of the modern age was addicted to progress and growth, but it is now crumbling. What was flashy and new a generation ago feels stale and tired today. And the search for the newer and better version of Christianity is a never-ending merry-go-round. A new world is emerging, one futurists, theologians, and philosophers call the age of postmodernism.

In his book *Soul Tsunami: Sink or Swim in the New Millennium Culture*, Leonard Sweet writes, "The seismic events that have happened in the aftermath of the postmodern earthquake have generated tidal waves that have created a whole new world out there."[3] The postmodern movement was birthed in the philosophical musings of the mid-twentieth century and gradually marked a shift from the Industrial Age to the "Age of Information." While modernity can be characterized as scientific, rational, and pragmatic, postmodernity can be described as experiential, spiritual, and communal. The paradigm shifts resulting from the transition from modernity to postmodernity that we are witnessing today can be comparable to previous shifts like the shift from Renaissance to Reformation or the advent of the Age of Reason.

As I mentioned in the introduction, we have been hearing alarming statistics for years about the steady flow of young people leaving the church in North America. According to the Pew Research Center, around one-third of young adults claim they have no religious affiliation. Often called the "nones" because of their disavowal of organized forms of religion,[4] they are currently the third largest religious group. If trends continue at the current rate, "nones" and other religions combined will outnumber Christians in America by 2024.[5] These are sobering statistics, indicating that massive cultural shifts are on the horizon for today's church.

We can blame these larger cultural shifts for the exodus of young people from the church, but we must also look to the culture to understand the values that are leading them away. In many ways, the lives of young adults—what they love, seek, and desire—have been shaped by the growth of technology, media, the global rise of terrorism, and shifting ideas about human sexuality and personal identity. These issues and many more are contributing to a growing skepticism about religious claims. While young adults will speak of being spiritual and spiritually interested, by and large they tend to distrust organized religion.

FROM POSTMODERN BACK TO PREMODERN

While the shift to postmodernism plays a significant role in shaping the emerging spirituality of young people, there are other shifts at work as well. We've moved from an age of certainty, where people willingly placed their trust in institutions and authorities, to an era of uncertainty. Today many young people are searching for truth that has been tested and tried, truth that acknowledges the holistic nature of the human person—addressing the heart, soul, mind, and body. Many are searching for this truth by looking not to the future but to the past. Looking beyond the modern age, they are looking to the *premodern* roots of our history.

This leads to an odd tension. As the shifts of postmodernism and individualism are leading people to reject authority and institutions, they are leaving a gaping hole. Young adults are sour on the promises of progress and science, tired of the latest and greatest, the ever-churning pursuit of the new. Thus, they are looking backward, away from our modern assumptions and rhythms, to reconnect with the human experience of those who have gone before us.

To understand the spirituality of young adults, we must recognize that while many are leaving the church behind, walking away entirely, a growing number of young adults are choosing a different path. While they are leaving behind a church they see as sold-out to modernity, they are choosing to embrace another form of the church, one with a different tradition and with different, far older practices and patterns of formation. Rather than looking for the new, they are returning to the old—even as they seek convergence between old and new and develop new approaches to ancient traditions. Everything old is becoming new again

At a recent conference, I sat down with a millennial believer who described his own encounter with some of the ancient church traditions. He said, "For my parents' generation, who were raised in church, tradition and liturgy were old and boring, but for our generation, liturgy is new, exciting, and fresh."

Author Rachel Held Evans is an example of a well-known millennial in this stream. Raised as an evangelical, she became critical of her evangelical roots, eventually leaving them behind to join the Episcopal Church. She chronicles her story in her recent book,

Searching for Sunday: Loving, Leaving, and Finding the Church. Her observations about evangelicalism are brutally honest, and whether you agree or disagree with her, they reveal how young adults are searching for something real and authentic, something they no longer believe the American evangelical church possesses:

> Millennials aren't looking for a hipper Christianity . . . We're looking for a truer Christianity, a more authentic Christianity. Like every generation before ours and every generation after, we're looking for Jesus—the same Jesus who can be found in the strange places he's always been found: in bread, in wine, in baptism, in the Word, in suffering, in community, and among the least of these.[6]

The search is a search for Jesus, and many young adults today aren't finding him in the typical church on the corner. To better understand what is missing, I asked professor and author James K.A. Smith why he believed young adults might be drawn to the liturgy of the historic church. He said:

> I think there are multiple factors. The first, and most funda-mental, I think, is that human beings are ritual animals. A lot of cultural forces in the church try to overwrite this, but our liturgical nature can't be effaced. So when people—perhaps especially young people—are given opportunities to inhabit the faith liturgically, it kind of plucks strings they didn't know they had. But I also think part of the draw is the very ancientness of these practices. The very strangeness carries a kind of transcen-dence they've never experienced in their big-box megachurch experiences, which feel like every other kind of "event" they've attended in their lives. They realize the church is older than their youth pastor. They might not know to name it this way, but I would say it is the *catholicity* that they are drawn by.[7]

Both Evans and Smith are inviting us to acknowledge two needs of today's younger believers: the need for authenticity and the need for a sense of belonging. Those who are attracted to liturgical expressions of the faith feel these practices allow them to "inhabit" the faith that has existed for over two thousand years. These practices also provide a sense of connection, to one another and to Christians throughout the ages. As Smith suggests, this idea of *catholicity* is vital, a longing for something lasting and universal that transcends our individual preferences and invites us out of ourselves into an experience of unity with others.

WHY YOUNG ADULTS ARE EMBRACING LITURGY

At this point you may be thinking, *This is all good, but what are the reasons that have led to this searching?* By interviewing young adults from across the United States, all of them from radically different Christian traditions, I've uncovered eight major reasons why a new generation is following the allure of liturgy. I won't claim that this list is exhaustive, but it does offer a succinct snapshot of the world of spirituality in North America (and across the pond).

Holistic Spirituality

The first yearning of young adults I've interviewed is for a *holistic*, or embodied, spirituality. In this age of technology and media, many young Christians have come to feel that the contemporary church (and even society as a whole) doesn't engage their faith in a holistic way. Many feel that churches focus on engaging only the mind or the heart. Some conservative evangelical churches tend to focus on teaching and preaching the Scriptures at the expense of the sacraments and other tactile expressions of the faith. This is somewhat a by-product of the Protestant Reformation, which elevated the preaching of the Word over the sacraments. At the other end of the spectrum, charismatic churches have tended to focus on emotions and experience at the expense of the mind. Liberal mainline churches have tended to focus on social-progressive issues, emphasizing causes rather than biblical teaching or emotive experiences. I've found that many young adults are looking for a faith that moves beyond these labels, transcending the "evangelical" or "charismatic," "liberal" or "conservative" divisions. They are seeking a holistic spirituality that embraces all aspects of their person—mind, body, and soul. Many are tired of the religious culture wars and would prefer to move past them in search of a holistic Christian faith that embraces the best of all sides.

For many, the culture war divisions evoke memories of interactions with others on the extreme edges, positions that don't acknowledge the full spectrum of Christianity. Young adults want a faith that not only engages the mind but involves the senses of touch, taste, and smell. The historic church has asserted that we are cleansed with the water of baptism, fed with the bread and wine of Communion, and healed by the laying on of hands using anointing oil. We are taught by the read-aloud Word, as well as with the colors of the sanctuary that correspond with the seasons of the Christian year. All these elements function *together* in the liturgical practices of the church and engage us holistically. Many young adults say these practices allow them to engage their whole person with the whole gospel.

A Sense of Mystery

Young adults are also drawn to historic practices because they long for a sense of mystery. It's impossible to ignore the brazen consumerism, combined with the media and technology, vying for our attention and our pocketbook. I remember visiting the Animal Kingdom at Walt Disney World and watching young children who were fascinated by the animatronics of robots while they couldn't care less about the exotic animals around them! But this is just a symptom of our reliance upon and cultural addiction to technology. We are drawn to the comfort, simplicity, and convenience technology provides, yet these tools have dulled our ability to appreciate the beauty and mystery of the real world around us.

The pragmatic consumerism that has infected the church leads us to value the elements of our faith and practice that are most "relevant" to us today. For example, many contemporary churches play worship music that echoes secular pop songs, and we've designed our church buildings to look like Walmarts or movie theaters, neglecting theologically informed architectural designs that were once popular in church buildings and sanctuaries. Young adults sense intuitively that today's churches have lost a vision for aesthetic beauty that encourages us to experience the mystery and transcendence of God. And they have grown tired of shallow, alternative approaches to the historic liturgical practices of past centuries. Young adults want more. They want depth and mystery, and they aren't afraid to say it. They are harboring a longing for a church that transcends any single culture, not an approach that simply accommodates the surrounding culture.

Commenting on liturgical expressions of the faith, Roman Catholic theologian and author of *Virtual Faith*, Tom Beaudoin, writes: "There is room for mystery. In fact, in their faith walk, today's youth often welcome mystery and sometimes are drawn to the mystical traditions of the Christian church. Meditative prayer, silence, ritual, and pilgrimage draw youth today."[8]

A Desire for Historical Rootedness

Today's young adults have grown up on fast food, video games, and smartphones. For many of them, divorce and remarriage was (and is) the norm. About 75 percent of the 1.2 million Americans who divorce each year eventually remarry, which means that many, like me, have grown up in blended homes. Others have moved several times during adolescence as a result of the changes and challenges of their home life. All of this has created a sense of *rootlessness*.

To counter the effects of transience and constant change, many are seeking to find a sense of stability by engaging with the roots of their faith. They are looking to the ancient history of the church and discovering that we are part of the larger family whose roots go back to the time of Christ. Many of those I've talked with have felt like spiritual orphans, people with no roots, no family history. They are discovering a new identity as they learn about their spiritual family heritage and embrace the origins of their faith in the Christian liturgical tradition. The experience is akin to a person discovering their family genealogy and suddenly realizing that they have deep family connections to the past. It's the realization that we are not independent Christians tied solely to our own time and place. We are part of the larger body of Christ, spanning continents and generations, a church that began not with the Reformation or the contemporary evangelical movement in America, but with Jesus Christ and the early church. Liturgical tradition offers young adults a refreshing alternative to the ahistorical culture of the modern evangelical church because it represents a place of belonging—one that has survived and thrived for over two thousand years.

Looking for a Countercultural Faith

Having grown up in a culture of entertainment and consumerism, many young people are now rejecting these cultural trends—or at the very least, they are uncomfortable with their presence in the church. For those who are looking for an opportunity to meet with God that cultivates an aura of transcendence, the rhythms of ancient liturgical worship are attractive. It's slow, repetitive, and it lacks instant gratification. The beauty of a faith that didn't start yesterday is that it is not driven by the latest fads or personalities. For many, it harkens to another time and is not bound to the biases of today's culture. One young adult from Chicago told me, "Liturgy is the opposite of our culture . . . in the sense that it provides ordered participation instead of watching passively. It's a way for the congregant to own what he or she is doing and saying. We live in an age where our opinions are voiced on social media—where we can read any opinion by typing something in on Google. So in this age, it is refreshing to stand for a faith with our whole being—words and actions."

Joshua Cockayne is in his late twenties and is currently doing research on corporate worship and liturgy at the Logos Institute for Analytic and Exegetical Theology at St. Andrews University in Scotland. Joshua belongs to the millennial generation and is researching liturgy, and specifically, how liturgy offers a structure and discipline for the spiritual life, something that is often lacking in the experience of many young adults. "While young adults often struggle to find routine and discipline in their private spiritual life," Joshua said, "liturgical worship can bring a much-needed focal point for a more disciplined spiritual life." He believes one reason the liturgical tradition resonates with young adults is its countercultural appeal:

> Some forms of liturgy also rail against the consumerist and individualist culture, which I think many millennials are keen to resist. There is a sense of belonging to something bigger and more important (for example, "we join with angels and archangels and all the company of heaven") which many young adults crave. The use of a set litany of Bible readings, for instance, speaks of the importance of wider and more difficult spiritual growth than some (potentially) more shallow forms of worship, which pick readings based on what people want to hear.

I believe Joshua is correct. Alongside a desire for the "new," there is a corresponding longing for the past, for a connection to something older and bigger than their individual tastes, interests, and experiences. There is an undercurrent in today's young adult culture that wants to retrieve the things of value from the past. Rather than being an "either/or," for many young adults, this is a "both/and."

Belonging to the Catholic (Universal) Church

Another reason many young adults are attracted to the liturgical forms of worship is because they are tired of the schisms and splits within Christianity. They see the liturgy as a pathway for unity, a way to unite us with the historic faith by inviting us to join the universal—little "c" catholic—church. In the liturgy, we participate in the same prayers, the same songs, and the same rhythms with Christians who have lived across the world and throughout the ages. Sadly, many Christians have spiritual amnesia and have forgotten or neglected the rich traditions and treasures of the faith from the past two thousand years. Historic liturgy offers us a way to correct our forgetfulness. Travis Collins, a worship leader from South Carolina who recently began helping his church practice liturgical worship, said, "[Liturgy] helps us remember that we are not alone. We are part of something much bigger and very beautiful. When we pray privately or corporately, we are joining our voices with millions of people around the world and with the heavenly host around the throne."

Liturgy offers a full, rich tradition of communal worship. While worship wars have led to division and disunity in the contemporary evangelical church, the fixed nature of liturgy and the decision to join in an existing tradition reminds us that we are a part of a larger family, one that has preceded us and will still be around when we are gone.[9] We are participating in the communion of the saints whose lineage runs from the time of Christ to the present-day church. Liturgy helps us remember that we are not independent from the body of Christ, from those who have gone before us. The Christian faith does not belong to us, as if we can change it to fit our likings and preferences. Nathan Smith, a twenty-something from Cincinnati, Ohio, shared some thoughts from his own faith journey that reflect this truth:

> Ultimately for me, to move to a liturgical emphasis was to move to a place of belonging. No longer do I feel absent from the history of my faith, nor do I feel that the existential longevity

of our religion rests on my evangelistic efforts. Instead, I have been given the utmost sense of freedom within the structure of the liturgy, and it connects me to the reality that God is bigger, more stable, and more gracious than I could remember on my own. It shapes for me a more beautiful picture of the Christ I take in weekly through the Eucharist.

Nathan is not alone. His words represent the longing many people today feel for both unity and rootedness.

Liturgy also connects us to the common prayer and worship of a *local* community of faith. The actual experience of the liturgy, celebrated each week with other brothers and sisters in a local context, unites us together in a shared expression of worship. We aren't praying different prayers, we are proclaiming aloud the same prayers that unite our hearts and minds together. Another student I interviewed said, "Liturgy gives the church rhythms to approach God corporately. There is something special about the body of Christ gathering to meet Jesus. As such, we as a people should not approach God as individuals, but as a family of God."

Sacramental Spirituality

While many Protestant low church traditions have all but abandoned the celebration and practice of the sacraments, some young adults are experiencing a resurgence of interest in learning about these sacred practices and the bounty of grace inherent within them. The sacraments offer a rich, multi-sensory worship experience that engages the whole person through touch, taste, and smell.

What is a sacrament? Traditionally, we speak of a sacrament as *an outward sign of an inward work of grace*. As Robert Webber defines it, "A primary meaning of 'sacrament' is that God works through his created order, through visible and tangible signs. For example, signs like bread, wine, oil, and laying on of hands are visible and tangible meeting points between God and people."[10] God chose the ordinary earthly objects of water, bread, and wine to be outward signs that sig-nify the deep spiritual realities of the kingdom of God. Young adults are longing for more than a faith that gives them head knowledge. They want a faith that is also tangible, engaging both the seen and unseen realities of life.

The Church's outward signs reveal to us a deeper dimension of the Christian faith, one that is often lacking in much of contempo-rary Christianity. Our faith is not an isolated, one-dimensional expe-rience that only impacts our hearts, souls, or minds. Instead, it must engage the whole of who we are, and the sacraments are an essential way in which God, through our faith, does this. Commenting on the attractional power of the sacraments, Rachel Held Evans writes, "The sacraments drew me back to church after I'd given up on it. When my faith became little more than an abstraction, a set of prop-ositions to be affirmed or denied, the tangible, tactile nature of the sacraments invited me to touch, smell, taste, hear, and see God in the stuff of everyday life again."[11] Liturgy leads us into a faith that holistically transforms us—our hearts, souls, minds, and bodies.

Gracious Orthodoxy

In the relativistic culture defined by a postmodern approach to questions of truth, many young adults yearn for boundaries, though they are not necessarily looking for exhaustive rules. They want an anchor for their faith, an embrace of beliefs that I would describe as a "gracious orthodoxy." What is a gracious orthodoxy? Several mil-lennials and Gen X young adults I talked with expressed a longing for "correct belief," yet they want to hold that belief in a way that is "full of grace." They want to stand up and confess the "faith once delivered to the saints," yet they reject dogmatic and exclusionary relationships with other Christians. They want a faith that broadly unites them with other Christians, even those who may be a part of other denominations and other traditions.

Often the young adults I interviewed spoke about the history of the church negatively, as a record of schisms over secondary doctrines. One person said, "I want to affirm what Christians have always believed in every age through a common faith and a common creed." This gracious orthodoxy is rooted in an ecumenical longing to affirm the historic, universal creeds of the church. They believe that by focusing on essentials of the faith, the creeds have the power to unite believers from different backgrounds instead of separating them. In chapter 3, we'll take a more in-depth look at the unitive power of Christian orthodoxy.

Finding an Anchor in Spiritual Practices

A final reason young adults are embracing liturgy is that the ancient practices of the church provide an anchor for their faith in a world of constant change. Many young people are longing for practices that help them consistently celebrate their faith. They were raised in churches that told them what to believe but didn't offer ways for them to practice their faith. Because we are creatures of habit, the habits we practice on a daily basis form us even if we are not aware of their power. Many of those returning to liturgy are hungry for time-honored practices that will form their faith and help them grow. Ancient practices help us develop roots that go deep whether we are young or old. In *Hungry Souls, Holy Companions*, Patricia Hendricks observes, "Today's young people welcome a return to the ancient practices which lead to a deep relationship with God."[12]

Joshua Cockayne, who I mentioned earlier, also makes this observation about spiritual practices: "In general, my experience is that young adults are seeking after a more holistic form of worship which engages not only their minds (as certain kinds of sermon-heavy worship might) but also their bodies and their emotions. Liturgy seeks to provide practices which shape the whole person and not just provide new ideas to be assessed."

Author and Anglican Bishop Todd Hunter calls this rediscovery of ancient practices a "repracticing." He writes, "When I embarked on a search to find ways to make the habits of Christianity and church significant and valuable, I used the old as a launching pad for repracticed new."[13] Many young people are incorporating these older practices in fresh new ways into their daily lives. They are using ancient practices such as the daily office, spiritual pilgrimage, *Lectio Divina*, and fasting as tools to help them grow deeper in their relationship with God.

MOVING FORWARD

In this chapter I've offered a broad survey of several ways young adults are rediscovering their faith. According to my observations, this rediscovering provides hope for traditional churches facing declining attendance and participation from younger members. It indicates that the prescription of relevance is not a fix for all that ails today's church. And it provides a hint that perhaps the future of the church isn't going to be found in trying to change the church to be more like the culture today, but in opening the treasure chest of the past and retrieving the beauty of church history. Could the future of the church lie in rediscovering our historical roots through ancient practices?

In many ways, the young adults I've spoken to from around the country are just a snapshot of a larger movement of Christians whose journeys of faith are leading them to recover historic practices that are rooted in liturgy. Building from this survey, we'll turn our attention now to specific examples of how young believers are recovering liturgy and living out their faith in a variety of different contexts. Our journey will take us across the country to meet many different young people, but before we do that, let's define what we mean by "liturgy."

REFLECTION QUESTIONS AND PRACTICES

- Chapter 1 explores eight reasons why young adults are exploring liturgy. Which reason stands out to you the most? Why?
- Why is it important that we understand the cultural influences that have led these young adults to embrace a more historic faith?
- In this chapter, I make a rather bold claim and state that the future of the church might lie in rediscovering our historic roots through ancient practices. What are your thoughts on this statement? In what ways do you agree or disagree?
- In what ways is liturgy countercultural to our usual consumeristic mindset? What is the value of this aspect, and in what ways might this be a hindrance for the church?

CHAPTER 2

THE POWER OF LITURGY

To be human is to be a liturgical animal,
a creature whose loves are shaped by worship.
JAMES K.A. SMITH

S eth Cain grew up in the Pentecostal tradition, and as a young adult had little exposure to worship experiences beyond that tradition. He knew there had to be more to church than his limited experience with contemporary Christian worship, and he felt a longing for something different. Due to his lack of exposure to other traditions, Seth increasingly felt the need to pursue a seminary experience that would broaden his understanding of the church and prepare him for faithful ministry rooted in the historic Christian faith. In 2002, he enrolled at Wheaton College, and at Wheaton he encountered the diversity he had hoped to see. Students and professors came from various church cultures and embraced practices from outside Pentecostal roots. While at Wheaton, Seth developed an interest in church history, and was especially fascinated by the historical progression of community practices. As these interests deepened, he sensed a growing hunger for a deeper connection to the larger body of Christ, a desire for his faith to be rooted both in the present and past work of God's Spirit.

One Sunday, a fellow student invited Seth and his wife, Ashley, to worship at a liturgical church near Wheaton. Having never experienced a traditional liturgical worship setting, both of them were curious, but they fully expected it to be a dull and formal experience of robotic recitations. Throughout the morning service, their preconceptions and defenses were slowly dismantled. The experience was entirely different from what they had expected.

Seth and Ashley described this first encounter with the liturgy as "completely reorienting." They were deeply moved to watch people prayerfully lining up to receive the Eucharist, some in tears, some deep in contemplation, and others with what they described as "visible, restful gratitude." That day was the beginning of a love affair with the beauty, reverence, and Christ-centeredness of the liturgical worship service. This encounter with liturgical worship transformed the direction of their life and ministry.

I share Seth's story because it leads us to address the questions we want to explore in this chapter. First, what is liturgy? When we speak of a liturgical service or tradition, what do we mean? And second, why does it seem to be resonating with many young adults today? Is there a reason for this interest, and if so, what is that reason? The answers to these questions can be found by examining the foundation of the Christian life: worship.

The word "worship," as it is used in the American church, is often synonymous with music and singing, but historically speaking, worship is far more than the songs we sing. Biblically defined, worship is the act of giving our whole selves back to God by demonstrating respect, reverence, honor, and glory toward him. God is worthy of our highest devotion, and he has called us to live all of life "for the praise of his glory" (Eph. 1:12). True worship of God begins in our hearts as we offer adoration, glory, and praise to God in a multitude of different ways. And yes, worship is manifested as we lift up our voices to God in prayer, praise, and song as well.

While it's helpful to begin by broadening our definition of

worship, we must also move beyond a merely mental understanding of worship and instead think of it as an embodied state. By "embodied" I mean that we, as living beings, must practice worship with more than just our minds and our lips. Worship is formative. In the songs we sing, the words we speak, and the thoughts we think, we are training our bodies to be disciples in every area of life—not just for an hour on Sunday. Worship prepares us to offer our entire lives to glorify God, and the liturgy of worship provides a tangible and interactive structure in which worship can freely occur.

WHAT IS LITURGY?

The English word "liturgy" comes from the Greek word *leitourgia,* which means "the work of the people." Throughout this book, I will be using the term "liturgy" in the broadest sense to refer both to something we do together in corporate worship *and* to individual spiritual disciplines, practices that help root us daily in the worship of God. Author Robert Mulholland reminds us of this twofold understanding of liturgy. He writes, "Liturgy consists of the corporate and individual patterns of devotion, worship, fellowship and obedience that enable us increasingly to manifest in the world God's kingdom of love, forgiveness, reconciliation, cleansing, healing and holiness."[1]

When we separate the corporate liturgy of a worship service from personal, individual liturgical practices, we create a false dichotomy. Why? Because they are connected. Private liturgical practices are rooted in the larger rhythms of corporate liturgy, and when I speak of liturgy, I'm referring to both these corporate and individual practices. The origin of liturgy comes from the practice of worship in the early church, and the purpose is to unite the body of believers in the essential work of the people—the worship of the one true God. Because liturgy provides an intentional way of fostering embodied worship, I think of it as essential vitamins for spiritual health, providing some of the nutrients that are missing from our contemporary worship services.

Maybe you are thinking, *This sounds great, but how is liturgy relevant for us today?* There are several ways to answer this question. I want to begin by looking at the lives of those who are embracing liturgy today and taking note of how this embrace is related to our emerging postmodern, individualistic culture. We'll begin by investigating several aspects that highlight the value of Christian liturgy and explain why young adults are drawn to it.

WHY DOES LITURGY RESONATE WITH PEOPLE TODAY?

Liturgy tells a story.

Liturgy is a re-enactment of the divine drama. It reminds us of the redemptive story of God and invites us to find our place within his narrative of redemption. As I noted earlier, there is something captivating about a good novel or play. In reading or watching a good story, the imagination is engaged. We enter into the narrative, and the liturgy is one way we can experience the story of God and meet the great Storyteller.

The Scriptures relate history as one grand narrative of God's redemptive love for lost humanity, and we find the good news of the gospel as the driving narrative of that story. It begins with creation and the tragedy of human sin and rebellion, and it continues to a dramatic point of conflict and resolution, with God sending his son Jesus Christ to die for our sins and rise victorious over evil and death. For centuries, authors and painters have used their talents to depict this narrative through art, writing, and song.

God's story helps us understand his true nature by focusing our hearts and minds on the message of his redemptive plan in such a way that it transforms and changes us. This is far more than simply grasping bare historical facts or embracing philosophical beliefs. History is full of amazing tales about great men and women of faith God has used to change the course of humankind and influence the world with the Word of God. Their lives were captured by the transformative power of God's story. They were drawn by it and drawn into it in such a way that their lives now form part of the unfolding narrative.

Sadly, as a result of the philosophical movements of the nineteenth and twentiethth centuries and the rise of individualism and a materialist understanding of the world, we now live in a story-deprived world. Ours is an age in which people don't know where they come from or where they are going. People today tend to focus on "the now" at the expense of the past, and we invest ourselves in what is temporal rather than what is eternal. As I mentioned, many contemporary Christians have historical "amnesia." They are missing vital aspects of the faith that are necessary for spiritual growth and maturity, and as a result they lack roots—an understanding of where they have come from and who they really are. Christians today have lost hold of our collective story, and that loss is one reason why liturgy resonates with so many. The recovery of liturgy offers them a way to re-enter the narrative, to re-engage with the story.

Liturgy speaks a powerful word into our postmodern identity crisis. Mark Galli writes, "The liturgy lives out a story in a story-deprived world. Liturgy is not a once-upon-a-time story we merely watch others perform. We are characters in this story, actors in the divine drama whose opening and closing has been written by Jesus Christ Himself."[2] Our contemporary lack of historical awareness can be partially remedied by reconnecting to the historic words, songs, and patterns practiced by Christians from generations past. This connection to the past, rooted in God's Word, help us to discover our own place in God's story. Through a beautiful blending of ancient foundations and a vision for the future, liturgical traditions offer a sense of belonging (connection) and a sense of purpose (meaning) by aligning our lives with the Christian narrative of redemption. As our hearts, minds, and bodies are formed by this narrative, it offers a fresh word to our present age. Liturgy frees us from having to create our own story from our limited perspective and experience.

Instead, it invites us to find our place and allows us to join an existing story, the story God has already written for his people.

Liturgy frees us from ourselves.

Liturgy helps us relinquish our desires to serve ourselves and invites us to surrender by selflessly serving God and others. How? By immersing our lives in God-centered worship on a regular basis. Liturgy is formative, retelling a story again and again that is holistically God-centered. It inoculates us from a man-centered experience of worship.

Much of contemporary Christian worship tends to focus on the individual. It is "me-centered," written and designed to emphasize how "I" feel or what I must do. It feeds our ego and our sense of self-importance, but these are not helpful or formative for following Jesus on the path of discipleship. Liturgy is designed to free us from the worship of self in order to focus our hearts on the triune God.

I recently encountered a student named Logan who left the Episcopal Church in which he had been raised for a more charismatic movement. Logan is now returning to his liturgical roots as he recognizes a longing for a deeper expression of his faith. He said, "The liturgy counterbalances the consumer culture we live in. It is so easy to build our lives with an egocentric ethos. The liturgy forces us to deal with this in terms of how we worship God." The counterbalance to our individualism happens as we engage in reading Scripture, reciting creeds, and verbalizing our confession in corporate and commonly shared liturgical rhythms. These refocus our adoration upon the almighty triune God and direct our attention away from ourselves.

Liturgy forms us.

Many young adults are drawn to liturgy because they are looking for resources to grow and deepen their discipleship. They have found in the liturgical rhythms and traditions something essential to their spiritual formation, a formative element that complements and enhances what they experience in private prayer and Scripture reading. They realize the benefits of including liturgy for both private and communal maturity.

Ever since its inception, the church has gathered for congregational worship to participate in the communal aspects of worship. As we come together week after week, we are slowly formed by the words, prayers, and sacred rhythms of the liturgy. The poetic words, the prayers, and the reading of Scripture leave an imprint upon our souls, and these practices shape us into men and women of God. The beauty of these rhythms is that they form us passively, almost without our knowledge. This formation is not contingent upon our mood or temperament when we enter the service. Simply by agreeing to participate and join with the existing structure and rhythms, liturgy has the power to change us.

The church has always recognized that formation takes place both communally and individually, and how we pray and worship corporately influences how we pray and worship individually. Before I discovered structured liturgy, my personal prayer life lacked rhythm, routine, and order. I had been trying to pray in my own strength, setting my own disciplines and structuring my own patterns, but consistency was difficult to maintain. Liturgy provided me with a new sense of stability, balance, and direction, something I had not previously known. The words and prayers of liturgy are scriptural and substantial, and although they are centuries old, the words are timeless and full of life and vitality. As I embraced the discipline of liturgical worship, I began to see transformation in my personal and private devotions. I experienced greater intimacy with God and began to sense a connection to the historic church and the experiences—and wisdom—of Christians from centuries past.

Liturgy sanctifies time.

In addition to drawing our attention away from ourselves and drawing us closer to one another in community, liturgy sanctifies our time. What do I mean by this? Most of us live our lives according to a secular calendar and work week, but liturgy reminds us that we belong to another time and place—the kingdom of God. Liturgy brings order and rhythm to our lives through the patterns of the *liturgical year* (sometimes referred to as the Christian calendar or church calendar). This annual cycle, patterned after the story of redemption in Christ, calls us out of our secular time and orders our lives around the life of Christ. By observing the seasons of the church, we live in contrast to the hustle and bustle of the world around us. During these seasons of celebration, anticipation, mourning, and reflection are times of fasting and times of feasting. In ordering our lives to this cycle, we acknowledge that life is rhythmic and that we were not made to strive for the success of the world that preaches excess and individuality at all costs. In submitting to these seasons, we acknowledge God's lordship in both the high and the low times of our lives.

The historic, annual rhythms of the church calendar were at one time quite new to me, and I know they can seem odd or unusual at first. It may help to understand some of the background of the liturgical calendar. The church began observing the various seasons of the gospel of Jesus Christ fairly early in its history. Churches in the Holy Land began developing liturgies to mark the days of Holy Week and Easter as ways of commemorating Jesus' life and death at specific holy sites. Pilgrims travelled to Jerusalem to participate in these ceremonies and eventually brought the practices back with them to their various countries. Over the centuries, the practice of following the Christian calendar spread, and today, many different Christian traditions remember the seasons of the Christian year.

The church year is an annual cycle including Advent, Epiphany, Lent, Easter, Pentecost, and what is referred to as Ordinary Time. Each season has its own unique set of prayers and themes that center our devotion and focus on the gospel of Jesus Christ and prepare us for another step on our journey of faith. Postmodern pilgrims have found that the rhythms of the church year can be a helpful aid to their own spiritual journey by reorienting their life around the life of Christ.

Each season brings with it traditions, and memories. The natural rhythms of spring, summer, fall, and winter—aligned with God's purposes in creation—can be powerful reminders of the seasonal rhythms of the spiritual life. In this way, they, too, function like a form of liturgy. Each season of the Christian year s reminds us of the multidimensional nature of growing in Christ. Knowing the liturgical calendar is important because daily and weekly liturgical worship revolves around the various seasons of the church year. In the words of liturgical scholar Massey Shepherd, "The Christian year is a mystery in which every moment and all times and seasons of this life are transcended and fulfilled in that reality which is beyond time."[3]

Liturgy is participatory.

Finally, perhaps the most powerful characteristic of liturgy is its *participatory* element. Many young adults have shared with me how they are tired of seeker-friendly, consumerist approaches to the faith in which they observe and absorb the work of others. They no longer want to be entertained; they want to participate. Liturgy ensures that each person has the opportunity to participate in the worship of the church, and it keeps us from being passive spectators who simply observe and consume knowledge. The rhythm of liturgy invites us to join in the story of God and, perhaps surprisingly, prevents our worship from becoming static or growing stale.

Nathan Hale, a millennial and former Southern Baptist, said, "There's a rhythm of back-and-forth in most liturgies that reminds us we're all engaged in the work of worship and brings us closer together as a community centered around the person of Jesus." Because it involves active participation, rather than passively sitting and watching, worshipers are placing themselves in a position to engage God's grace as he transforms their hearts, minds, and bodies.

The participatory nature of liturgical worship involves innumerable expressions that invite us to engage our entire bodies in different movements and posturing. During a liturgical service, you will notice people standing, sitting, kneeling, and making various gestures throughout the service. While some might find this strange, it is yet another way in which the liturgical structure of worship involves our bodies as well as our minds and emotions. For many young adults who are used to sitting and receiving in a worship service, liturgy calls them out and offers depth and substance. Young adults discover a sense of belonging, and a concreteness and purpose they cannot manufacture themselves or find in the production-oriented worship services of today's contemporary churches.

THE FOURFOLD PATTERN OF THE LITURGY

To this point we've talked about the *why* of liturgy. Now, let's look at the *how* of liturgy. We'll begin by focusing on the structure of liturgy.

There are historic and theological reasons for how the liturgy is laid out. Many contemporary Christians leaders may be tempted to cut and paste some of the traditional practices of the church into various places in a modern worship service, but this approach of "blending," while it can be done well, also carries several risks. There is a danger of removing elements of the traditional church liturgies from their structure and context, stripping them of their formative power and influence. Liturgist Patrick Malloy cautions individuals and churches against adopting ancient patterns of the liturgical tradition without understanding the beliefs that lie behind them. He writes, "This has led to a liturgical style that embraces experience but, as some within the movement acknowledge, lacks theological grounding."[4] Exploring liturgical practices without understanding the original context can idolize the method rather than embracing true God-centered worship.

To dig a bit deeper into the structure of liturgy, let's explore a typical four-part pattern—gathering, hearing, feeding, and sending—to attempt to understand how liturgy's structure forms those who participate in communal worship. The structure of most liturgy offers an invitation to those who are on a journey of worship, asking them to join in the story of God through worshiping in song, hearing the Scriptures, listening to a sermon, remembering the life, death, and resurrection of Jesus at the Communion table, and being sent back into the world in mission. This fourfold pattern offers a unique yet simple way to structure a worship service and can be adapted to any context of worship, whether ancient or modern.

Gathering

At the heart of our shared humanity is our need for community. Regardless of whether you are an introvert or an extrovert, we are all born with a need for human connection. We see this need in Genesis, as from the very beginning Adam and Eve are created to relate to one another and to God. What, then, could be more natural than gathering with others, especially those whom we love? In this sense, liturgy is more like a family dinner than a worship service. It provides a place for connection among God's people. The first part of the service begins with believers gathering from around the city to worship God in song and prayer.

The focus on coming together to connect around a common love and desire for Jesus speaks deeply to the young adults I've encountered. As one of my students so eloquently shared with me, "The liturgy gives the church a rhythm to corporately approach God as a family. There is something special about the body of Christ gathering to meet Jesus. I've come to see that we approach God in our worship as a family." The early church met in people's homes, and it was the understanding of the church as a family of God's people that formed its identity. This "family" identity is something the liturgy seeks to form and shape in us as well.

Over time, Christians began to worship in church buildings to accommodate larger gatherings of believers, but despite this significant shift, gathering together in worship reminds us that the church is still a family of believers, not a collection of isolated individuals living life alone. Regardless of the size or space, the gathering portion of the liturgy brings believers together to worship and glorify the risen Christ as a unified community. Simply put, we don't worship God alone.

Today, this gathering together in worship can happen in a variety of ways. Some churches use a time at the beginning of the service for informal greetings and opening prayer to call the people to worship, while other churches may start with an organ prelude, choir processional, or a contemporary praise chorus. It is common for churches to blend traditional hymns and contemporary worship songs as a part of their gathering entrance. Gathering for worship doesn't have to fit within the confines of a traditional church building. In fact, over the last few years, I have been able to worship in churches around the world—in cities, in jungles, and on top of mountains. The gathering calls the people of the church out of the world, brings them before God to worship, reminds them of their connection to one another as the body of Christ, and prepares them to hear the Word of the Lord.

Hearing

Some of my earliest memories include sitting around listening to my parents and grandparents telling family stories. These stories captivated my imagination and gave me a greater understanding of who I am in relation to the rest of my family. Storytelling has often served as a way for me to understand my identity and how I'm related to others. Telling stories is an art form as old as time itself, and over the centuries it has served as the foundation of religions, empires, and organizations alike, a catalyst that shapes identities and unites people. Think about how the stories of history have shaped our culture today. This is one reason why the second part of liturgy—hearing—is so transformative. It is where we proclaim the story of God for all to hear.

In a liturgical service, the story of God is retold primarily through the reading aloud of the Scriptures, the recitation of prayers, and responsive readings. These readings usually include passages from the Old Testament, a psalm, something from the Epistles, and a passage from the Gospels. Saturating the service with the Scriptures, drawing from both the Old and New Testaments, ensures that the Word of God is the foundation of worship. During the reading of the Word, we sit, listen, reflect, and remember that we belong to a story larger than ourselves. This posture of receiving the Word of God forms us because we hear the Word of God and the Spirit applies its truths to our hearts and minds.

Hearing various passages of Scripture read aloud back-to-back can seem overwhelming or even boring at first. Over time, as a congregation begins to immerse itself in Scripture, the congregants will find they are formed and shaped by the narrative being communicated. I recently experienced this in a memorable way at an Easter Vigil service in Lexington, Kentucky. The Easter Vigil is a powerful liturgical service for me, one filled with the drama of light and darkness and the reading of lengthy passages of Scripture. The appointed passages walk the congregation from the creation account all the way through the life and resurrection of Jesus Christ. As I sat and listened with my ears, I had an overwhelming sense of the continuity of the Bible, and by hearing it all read at one time, I began to picture myself as a part of this larger gospel story.

Following the service, I sensed that in addition to the listening I'd done with my ears, I had been listening with the ears of my heart. Even passages that might appear mundane on the surface have had a transformative effect on me, revealing the power of the proclaimed Word of God.

Another way the liturgy is "heard" is through the preaching of a sermon based on one of the passages of Scripture that was just read. The goal of the sermon is to apply the Word to everyday life. John Stott reminds us of an important truth about this: "Preaching is indispensable to Christianity. Without preaching, a necessary part of its authenticity has been lost. For Christianity, in its very essence, is a religion of the Word of God."[5] Stott is right on the mark here, and in conducting my own research I have heard many stories of how the Lord has used a sermon to speak to someone about the condition of their soul, giving them a word of encouragement needed in a particular moment.

After the sermon, the congregation affirms its faith by reciting the words of either the Nicene Creed or the Apostles' Creed. The historic creeds offer a concise summary of authentic Christian beliefs and further add to the narrative of the service by offering a foundation of doctrine. These doctrinal statements contain essential Christian beliefs, tied to the Christian story (e.g., the resurrection, the divinity of Christ, the virgin birth, and the Trinity). The creeds represent the beliefs long-held by the majority of Christians. Reciting the creeds reminds us that through our common faith in these essentials, we can find common ground in our shared stories of faith, offering a measure of unity with Christians of other denominations and backgrounds. The creeds guard the faith, protecting the unity of the church, but they do not limit the leading of the Holy Spirit. They ground our faith and allow us to worship God together while allowing for both unity and diversity.

After a recitation of the creeds is often a time called the "Prayers of the People" or "Prayers of the Faithful." This is a time during which the congregation prays together for the church, the world, and those in need. The prayers usually embrace a historic form of intercessory prayer called the litany or "bidding prayer." This is where the person leading the prayer time makes a specific request to God, and the people who are gathered respond with a sentence or phrase, such as "Lord, hear our prayer" or "Lord, have mercy." The Prayers of the People bring everyone together around the needs of the world, the needs of the church, and the concerns of the local community. This time is an opportunity for a single, local church body to reflect upon the needs of others and spiritually connect with the universal church.

Following the Prayers of the People, the liturgy usually provides the congregation a time for confession of sins before God and one another. This is a time of corporate confession of sins about "what we have done and what we have left undone," which is followed by a pronouncement of absolution. Ins some ways, this is the "altar call" of the liturgical service, a time which provides a space for everyone to confess their sins before God and receive forgiveness and pardon. Here is one example of a corporate confession found in the Anglican *Book of Common Prayer*:

> *Most merciful God,*
> *we confess that we have sinned against you*
> *in thought, word, and deed,*
> *by what we have done,*
> *and by what we have left undone.*
> *We have not loved you with our whole heart;*
> *we have not loved our neighbors as ourselves.*
> *We are truly sorry and we humbly repent.*
> *For the sake of your Son Jesus Christ,*
> *have mercy on us and forgive us;*
> *that we may delight in your will,*
> *and walk in your ways,*
> *to the glory of your Name. Amen.*

Following the confession of sin, the absolution reminds the congregation that God is a God of grace, always ready to forgive us of our many sins. Having been forgiven, the congregation then greets one another with a sign of peace, often called "the passing of the peace." This is not only a time to greet one another, but also an opportunity to remember our peace with God and with one another. These practices of confession and peace remind us that we not only need to receive forgiveness, we need to give it away. We should freely forgive others as God has freely forgiven us. Practicing forgiveness is important because Jesus gives significant attention to the importance of forgiving others: "For if you forgive others their trespasses, your heavenly Father will also forgive you, but if you do not forgive others their trespasses, neither will your Father forgive your trespasses" (Matt. 6:14–15 ESV). God wants to bring healing and restoration to our broken relationships, and one of the beauties of the liturgy is that it gives us physical practices like these that embody spiritual realities.

Through each of these elements, the truths of God's story are proclaimed for the whole congregation to hear. The practices of hearing constitute not only the basic beliefs of Christianity, but also the personal nature of our redemption and our need for the grace and love of God. The proclamation of these powerful truths demands a response, of course. This leads us to the next segment of the common liturgical rhythm: celebrating the gifts of God through Communion.

Feeding

I love to eat! In fact, one of my favorite things is trying out new foods, especially foods from other cultures. Over the last few years, I have travelled to twelve countries on four continents, and I've learned that one of the most common human practices across all cultures is the sharing of meals. Eating is universal—no matter where you are from, you have to eat! Regardless of our cultural background, eating a meal with others represents a fundamental connection between human beings who want to grow in relationship. Few places are better for building relationships than the dinner table. Eating together naturally fosters community, friendship, and trust.

Patterned after this created reality, the liturgical service leaves room for the power of a meal within the experience of worship. At the heart of the liturgy is a meal served at the Lord's Table, a meal known as the Lord's Supper, Communion, or the Eucharist. It's a meal shared in response to hearing the story of the plight of creation and God's offer of grace and redemption to humanity. In the meal, the congregation comes forward to receive the grace of God through Communion with God and one another at the table.

This is the church's act of remembering the death of Jesus Christ and anticipating his second coming by eating small pieces of bread (or wafers) and wine. Hearing the Word prepares us to come to the Lord's Supper, and the meal itself offers us a way to respond tangibly to the message of God's Word and the grace preached within it.

The importance of the Lord's Table can be traced back to its vital role in the early life of the church. The early church celebrated Communion every time they came together to worship, and in some cases, they practiced it daily.[6] In the book of Acts, we can see that the life of the early church revolved around fellowship. At the heart of the Greek word for fellowship (*koinonia*) is the idea of participation. *Koinonia* is used to describe both the fellowship and actual participation in the Lord's Supper.[7] No single word in the English language fully captures the meaning of this Greek word. It's more than just a shared experience and nice conversation with other people. It is, at the deepest level, a spiritual connection in Christ, a supernatural bond provided by God's grace. This idea of fellowship is important for understanding what it means to live the sacramental life, and it is one of the reasons why young people are drawn to liturgy. The Christian life is rooted in living together in community, sharing life with one another and with Christ. We encounter the triune God in and through the regular worship of the church and in our participation in the Lord's Supper.

The early Christians viewed the Communion meals of *koinonia* as absolutely vital to their life as a church. In Acts 2:42, we read, "They devoted themselves to the apostles' teaching and to the fellowship, to the breaking of bread and to prayer." The "breaking of bread" (a reference to the Lord's Table) was a continual reminder of what Christ had done for them. It was also a reminder of God's ongoing presence and activity in the Church—past, present, and future. The Eucharist (or "the thanksgiving") became the center of their worship together because it was an act of remembrance and a reminder of the future coming of Christ's final victory. The Greek word for remembrance is *anamnesis,* which means a recollection of the past that enlivens and empowers the present. It is more than just a mental activity of individuals thinking about the past; it speaks to the ritual and verbal activity of communities.[8] For the early Christian community, the habits of remembrance and thanksgiving created a holistic approach to spirituality that celebrated God's holy presence in, with, and among them as they came together.

Throughout the ages, Holy Communion has typically been the climax of the liturgical worship gathering. At the Lord's Table, Christians are invited to partake of consecrated bread and wine. They are welcome to the table with the words, "The gifts of God for the people of God." As the congregation comes forward to the table at the front of the worship space and partakes of the bread and the wine, it embodies what heaven will be like—the union of God's people as one at Christ's table. At the table of the Lord, our differences no longer define us. Young, old, black, white, rich, and poor, are all welcome. The Lord's Table is the family table where all of God's children come and dine.

Sending

Finally, after gathering as the family of God and sharing a meal at the Lord's Table, the priest or worship leader blesses the congregation and sends it back into the world on mission through the *benediction.* At the conclusion of the traditional Eucharist service of the ancient church, the priest would pray the benediction, *Ite, missa est,* meaning, "Go, you are sent." The word *missa* is the Latin word for mission and is where we get the modern term "mass," often used in reference to a Roman Catholic worship gathering. The liturgy gathers us together to worship the triune God and then prepares us to go back out into the world on his redemptive mission.

The important thing to note here is that worship and mission are inseparably linked. As N. T. Wright says, "The link between worship and mission is so close that many prefer to speak of them in terms of each other. Glad, rich worship of God revealed in Jesus invites outsiders to come in, welcomes them, nourishes them, and challenges them. . . . Thus, though I continue to speak of worship and mission as separate activities, I also insist on integrating them."[9] As the body of Christ, we come together to worship God *in order to be sent back out into the world through mission.* Then we invite others into the life of worship, and the cycle starts over again.

A GROWING INTEREST

Perhaps you opened this book because you are interested in something more than what the contemporary church worship service has to offer. Many churches today, with their smoke machines and laser light shows, have replaced these traditional practices and patterns of worship with other elements or practices. What we need to understand is that regardless of what we do in worship, it is formative, and the songs we sing, the things we say, and the responses we offer all shape us in some way. If reading this brief introduction to the fourfold structure of liturgy has stirred some interest in you, the good news is that you are not alone. Many people of all ages have found an oasis in the desert in the liturgical worship tradition. The ancient practices and rhythms of liturgy have been a treasure hidden in our postmodern society. In later chapters, we are going to look at different types of liturgical churches to give you a taste of what the liturgy can look like—some very old and some very new. Come and see how churches today are engaging a new generation with these traditional elements of the liturgy.

REFLECTION QUESTIONS
AND PRACTICES

- I begin with the quote by James K.A. Smith, *"To be human is to be a liturgical animal, a creature whose loves are shaped by worship."* In what ways do you agree or disagree with this statement?
- In this chapter, Seth and Ashley Cain describe their encounter with liturgy as completely reorienting their understanding of faith and ministry. What might it mean for your life and faith to be reoriented by liturgy?
- What do you think about the definition of liturgy as "the work of the people," and how does this definition relate to the appeal of liturgy to young adults?
- How does dividing corporate liturgy from individual liturgical practices create a false dichotomy?
- Based on what you read in this chapter (especially in light of the fourfold order of worship), how does liturgy invite us into the story of redemption?

CHAPTER 3

SURPRISED BY ORTHODOXY

Orthodoxy thrives in pluralism.
ANDY CROUCH

Gary Ball is a surfer from Santa Cruz, California, who now serves as an Anglican pastor in Asheville, North Carolina. A surfer and an Anglican—sounds like an oxymoron, doesn't it? That's because we associate surfing with the rejection of rules and structure, the antithesis of a traditional, liturgical church. Surfer culture is an expression of free living, a culture that allows people to fully embrace spontaneity. In addition to being a surfer, Gary was involved in several churches with a non-creedal, evangelical worshiping tradition—all prior to becoming an Anglican pastor. For most of his life as a follower of Christ, spontaneity was one of Gary's defining characteristics. So what would lead a surfer like Gary, whose life embraced spontaneity, into joining a liturgical tradition that embraces structure and order?

The simple answer is that it was the structure and order that drew him in. It was the liturgical tradition's ability to articulate a clear and concise picture of belief that played a vital role in why he embraced it. "People are leaving other denominations today because they don't know who they are," he said. "In the liturgy, our identity is shaped through worship, which also counteracts our culture's trend toward individualism. When we gather for worship on Sunday mornings, there is a corporate confession and a corporate affirmation of faith." In his testimony, I heard him speak about the value of embracing a creedal faith as well, one that has a clearly defined and concise proclamation of what the church believes.

This corporate confession and affirmation of the faith is rooted in the historic creeds of Christianity, especially the Apostles', Athanasian, and Nicene Creeds. The Nicene Creed for example, begins with the words, "We believe in one God." In an age of relativism and individualism, what could be more counter-cultural for a young adult than a corporate affirmation of a faith that is over 1,500 years old? The big question being asked today isn't, "Do you believe in God?" but *"Which* God do you believe in?"

There are hundreds of religions in North America, not to mention thousands of Christian denominations, many of which do not explicitly embrace concrete, creedal statements of orthodoxy (such as the Apostles' Creed). In a choose-your-own-religion culture of abounding options, where can young people find something that calls them beyond their own preferences or opinions? What can connect and ground them to a historic faith, one shared by generations past? The historic creeds are surprisingly popular among a new generation of believers. I've heard countless stories of individuals excited to discover these rich treasures, embracing them for their own spiritual growth and discipleship.

WHERE WILL THEY LAND?

Young adults who have grown up in a postmodern world are seeking "spirituality" wherever they can find it. Even among those who have grown up in the Christian church, there is often only a vague understanding of what Christians actually believe. Sociologists Christian Smith and Melinda Lundquist Denton have examined the spiritual lives of youth and shared the result in their book *Soul Searching: The Religious Lives and Spiritual Lives of American Teenagers.* Their findings indicate that the majority of youth adhere to a vague understanding of religion, a set of beliefs that are not necessarily Christian, something they call Moralistic Therapeutic Deism (MTD).[1] MTD has five basic tenets:

1. A God exists who created and orders the worlds and watches over human life on earth.
2. God wants people to be good, nice, and fair to each other, as taught in the Bible and by most world religions.
3. The central goal of life is to be happy and to feel good about oneself.
4. God does not need to be particularly involved in one's life except when he is needed to resolve a problem.
5. Good people go to heaven when they die.[2]

Again, notice how vague these statements are, especially when compared to the historic affirmations of creedal Christianity. Moral and religious relativism has infiltrated the church and profoundly influenced the religious thinking of many young people. Thankfully, in some cases they are responding to this relativism in positive ways. Instead of embracing these nebulous and rootless beliefs, they are looking for firm ground on which to stand. Because they have not been introduced to creeds, confessions, and catechisms in the youth programs or discipleship ministries of their church, they are turning to other Christian traditions that embrace liturgy and creedal affirmations.

Even though the broader trend is somewhat discouraging, the response of young adults like Gary, who are embracing Christian orthodoxy through the historic liturgical tradition, is encouraging and offers a measure of hope. In an article for *The American Conservative,* writer Gracy Olmstead says the movement toward a liturgical expression of faith indicates a search for meaning that permeates the postmodern era.[3] In contrast to the modern era with its reliance upon certainty, the postmodern era has all but done away with certainty in favor of plurality and relativism, but this has proven to be an empty pursuit for many. As they encounter the uncertainty and ambiguity of a postmodern world, young people are beginning to look for something to believe in again, something that adds stability to their identity. A creedal faith offers them this clear, stable foundation.

Colleen Carroll Campbell is an author, journalist, former presidential speechwriter, and Roman Catholic who has observed this movement since the late 1990s. In 2000, she won a Phillips Journalism Fellowship, which allowed her to spend a year researching for her book, *The New Faithful*, a look at why some young adults are embracing Christian orthodoxy. She writes, "Amid the swirl of spiritual, religious, and moral choices that exist in American culture today, many young adults are opting for the tried and true worldview of Christian orthodoxy."[4] Campbell goes on to offer several key characteristics of young adults who are embracing orthodoxy:

- Their identity is centered on their religious beliefs, and their morality derives from those beliefs.
- They are attracted to a worldview that challenges many core values of the dominant secular culture while addressing their deepest questions and concerns. Time-tested teachings and meaningful tradition speaks to them.
- They embrace challenging faith commitments that offer them firm guidance on how to live their lives.
- They yearn for mystery and tend to trust their intuitive senses that what they have found is true, real, and worth living to the extreme.
- They strive for personal holiness, authenticity, and integration in their spiritual lives and are attracted to people and congregations that do the same. Conversely, they are repelled by complacency, hypocrisy, and pandering.

- Their beliefs and practices—though usually completely compatible with the core tenets of their faith traditions—often defy conventional wisdom about their generation, the expectations of religious leaders, and existing classifications of believers within individual denominations (for example, charismatic or conventional, liberal or conservative).
- They are, for the most part, concerned with impacting and engaging the larger culture. Yet they are equally committed to living out their beliefs in the context of authentic communities that support them and hold them accountable.[5]

Campbell's findings confirm what I have found in my own conversations and interviews with young adults across the country. In the next section, I'd like to build upon Campbell's summary to explore the nature of Christian orthodoxy and why it matters—especially to today's young adults. I believe there are two primary reasons why young people are drawn to the historic Christian faith: the *certainty* and the *identity* that's found within community.

THE ALLURES OF CERTAINTY AND COMMUNAL IDENTITY

Today's young adults have grown up in an age of political, financial, moral, and global uncertainty. While some are comfortable swimming in the uncertain waters of postmodernity with all of its relativity and flexibility, others have found those waters hazardous to their personal and spiritual health. These young people are searching for truths that transcend their immediate context. They long to be part of something lasting, and many have found that certainty in expressions of the Christian faith that embrace and acknowledge the full scope of church history—a Christian tradition that goes back two thousand years. This is not an uncritical embrace of the past. Yet even if they don't agree with everything the church taught or practiced in those two thousand years, they are finding a renewed sense of certainty and continuity by affirming their embrace of the "faith once delivered for all the saints" (Jude 1:3 NKJV).

Author and blogger Ben Irwin states, "I don't always believe the words of the Nicene Creed. But I say them anyway. Sometimes they're more of a confession of *desire* than *conviction*, a statement of what I desperately hope to be true."[6] Young adults are longing for something to believe in and a story to be a part of, and for many, the liturgical tradition provides them with that sense of stability, a solid anchor amidst the uncertainty of their own struggles and the transitions of postmodern culture.

A second and similar benefit young adults are finding in historic orthodoxy is that it offers them an identity within a rooted community. With the rising influence of technology in our culture, young people are more "connected" than ever before, but they are not fooled by technological claims offering a superior alternative to face-to-face community. Instead, we are learning that the so-called "connectivity" of today—while it does have benefits—also has costs and drawbacks. When technology is used in lieu of physical interaction, it can lead to the disintegration of genuine friendships, replacing them with artificial projections of what people want others to see. Studies have consistently found that the rise of technology among young people has not brought happiness and has made them more lonely and depressed than ever before.[7] Being a part of a rooted, face-to-face community and forming deep relationships with others remains crucial to our health and well-being. The biblical narrative of Genesis reminds us that we weren't created to be alone, and we flourish when we are able to be vulnerable and open with both God and those around us. Liturgical traditions, when they are rooted in historic movements and denominations, offer the type of identity only a committed community can provide—the kind of identity young people today are seeking.

We are inherently social beings, and we find aspects of our identity in and through the communities in which we belong. The traditions of those communities give us a common language, common beliefs, and a common worship, all of which binds us together through shared experiences. Again, Ben Irwin shares how the traditional church has helped his faith: "When I struggle to believe, the rhythms and patterns and prayers of the liturgy are like an anchor. It's as if the rest of the community—those around me and those who came before me—are saying, 'It's OK. We'll carry you through this part.'"[8] In a similar way, a twentysomething named Rebecca from Cincinnati, Ohio, told me, "There is such a beautiful inter-webbing of the liturgy within the church's understanding of its beliefs. It grounds the worshiping church body in a common and one voice to God. I think this matters a great deal, it unites many people and brings the church body into the same stream and same voice." The words of the historic liturgy and the words of the creeds unite us with others worshiping in our local congregations, with those who are saying the same words around the world, and with those who have gone before us. When we participate in liturgy, we are a part of a global and historic community, and this provides a deep sense of connectedness and belonging far greater than the transient connections of technology.

These driving needs for certainty and community shape our identity, and young people are tapping into this need. In response to their uncertainty, creedal expressions of faith empower them to proclaim with confidence the beliefs of the church. The continuity between what has been believed in generations past to the present today, together with a community in which to belong, powerfully transforms and shapes both group and individual identities. By participating in liturgical expressions of the Christian faith, these young people are not only discovering ancient roots; they are finding themselves as well.

WE BELIEVE, BUT WHY DOES IT MATTER?

So why does historic orthodox belief matter? About fifteen years ago, I was the founding pastor of a church in North Carolina. Our church had loud music, we used stage lighting, and we served coffee. We were your typical, contemporary American church. Within a short time, the church outgrew the home where we were meeting, and we numbered several hundred people. The growth brought several new challenges and opportunities. Many of the new people who began attending had little to no church background and knew nothing about Christianity. Needless to say, it was a bit messy at the beginning! One of our biggest challenges was figuring out how to help new believers learn the basics of the faith. We realized the essential nature of discipleship for the health and survival of new Christians and the ongoing life of the church. Consequently, we began to shift our focus to spiritual growth by developing disciples instead of simply growing our church by adding more attendees.

This all sounds great in theory, but practically, I was faced with a question: *What was I going to teach these new believers?* It's easy to embrace the "strategy" of discipleship, but I didn't have a clue how to implement this in practice. Like most young pastors, I turned to the latest books, programs, and curriculum to convey the essentials of the faith, but I found they either lacked substance or were too academic. They were written at a level beyond what the normal person attending our church could understand. It was discouraging! I was looking for a discipleship tool that could help real people connect with real doctrine in a simple, yet transformative way.

Then it happened.

I stopped looking for the next big thing, the latest curriculum. I began looking backward, to the pages of church history, for answers to my questions. I read books, biographies, and devotionals, and I kept coming across references to the Apostles' Creed. At first, I failed to grasp the contemporary relevance of the creed because it seemed so ordinary and basic. Yet as is often the case, it's the ordinary things in life, the things we overlook and take for granted, that are most formative and useful. Think about the basic essentials a person needs for everyday life. How different would your life be if you didn't have a roof over your head, food to eat, air to breathe? How often do we overlook or under appreciate these essential things?

I believe we do something similar with the historic creeds of the church. We have become so consumed with what the church *does,* looking for new and better models and practices, that we forget who the church *is,* neglecting the core tenets of our faith. As I began to read and reflect on the Apostles' Creed, I began to see its relevance for today's believers as a useful tool for discipleship.

THE IMPORTANT PLACE OF ORTHODOXY

What we believe shapes our identity, and ultimately, who we are. Singer-songwriter Rich Mullins affirmed this in an older song called "Creed." In the words of the song, he writes: "And I believe what I believe is what makes me what I am. I did not make it, no it is making me. It is the very truth of God, and not the invention of any man." Orthodoxy means "right belief," and for Christianity, a right belief is a belief that agrees with the whole of Scripture and the teachings of Jesus and the apostles. This is especially true regarding the core doctrines of the Trinity and the church. What makes Christian orthodoxy stand apart in our postmodern world is its clear statements of what we believe, and the commitment to hold to these beliefs regardless of the relativism we find in the world. While others may abandon their beliefs for the latest trends, Christians are rooted, holding firm, concrete beliefs about the Triune God: Father, Son, and Holy Spirit.

Our orthodoxy—right beliefs—are important for discipleship because orthodoxy is directly connected to our *orthopraxy,* our "right action." The practical application of a belief is an action taken in response to or based on that belief. This is why what we believe about God matters immensely. What we believe about God influences how we think, pray, worship, and, ultimately, how we live. No, we are not all called to be professional theologians, but every Christian has a responsibility to know what they believe for themselves. You can't worship what you don't know.

So, what *do* Christians believe? Well, in one sense, Christians simply believe what has been taught in the Holy Scriptures and the historic creeds and councils. Christianity is unified by its center, not by its boundaries. These "essentials" are what C. S. Lewis had in mind when he wrote his book *Mere Christianity* "to explain and defend the belief that has been common to nearly all Christians at all times."[9] The essentials are what author G. K. Chesterton believed should be "understood by everyone calling himself Christian until a very short time ago and the general historic conduct of those who held such a creed."[10] Since the earliest of times, Christians have believed the teachings of the Bible and recited the creeds during times of prayer and worship to remind them of the faith they professed, the faith handed down to the apostles and guarded by the church to the present day.

Rather than reinventing the faith, young people are drawn back to the foundational truths of Christianity, back to orthodoxy. I believe every generation of believers must revisit the faith and doctrines of the early church as found in the Holy Scriptures and the historic creeds. In our time, these truths and doctrines sharply contrast with the postmodern mood of our culture, providing a new or young Christian with a substantial foundation upon which to stand. The mission of the church is to engage a changing world with an ancient faith that is relevant and fresh for each generation. It's about communicating clearly and calling each generation to the solid foundation of orthodoxy.

TELLING GOD'S STORY THROUGH THE CREEDS

Perhaps all this talk about the creeds has you wondering, *What are the creeds, and how many of them are there?* A creed is a brief statement of faith used to summarize biblical teaching, clarify doctrinal points, and distinguish truth from error. The word *creed* comes from the Latin word *credo*, meaning, "I believe," and these statements have played a crucial role in the life of the church. In fact, the Bible contains a number of creed-like passages (see Deut. 6:4–9; 1 Cor. 8:6, 15:3–4; 1 Tim. 3:16).

There are three commonly accepted creeds of the Christian church—the Apostles' Creed, the Nicene Creed, and the Athanasian Creed. All three offer a concise, carefully nuanced summary of authentic Christian beliefs and definitions of essential Christian doctrines (e.g., the divinity of Christ, the virgin birth, and the Trinity) commonly held by the majority of Christians through the centuries. It is through our common acceptance of these essentials that Christians can seek unity with other Christians, even across cultural and denominational divides. Our creeds guard the faith from error, but they do not limit the leading of the Holy Spirit. The common ground of faith established by the creeds allows us to move forward together into the world to fulfill the mission of God. Because of their importance, the language of the creeds is often found sprinkled throughout historic prayers, liturgies, ceremonies, and catechisms. In many ways, the creeds act as an anchor, providing a doctrinal foundation for the church.

Here is a closer look at the three major creeds, along with a summary of the value that some young adults find in them as a resource for discipleship and spiritual growth.

The Apostles' Creed

The Apostles' Creed is the most concise creed, detailing beliefs observed by Christians everywhere. As the early church spread, it needed a practical statement of faith to help believers focus on the essential doctrines. Even though there is no historical evidence of this, the creed is traditionally attributed to the apostles. However, the Apostles' Creed is called such, not because the original apostles wrote it (which is unlikely), but because *it accurately reflects the teaching of the apostles—the apostolic faith.* The earliest form of the Apostles' Creed appeared around the second century, and it assumed its final form sometime in the eighth century.

The Nicene Creed

As the church continued to grow and expand, heresies also grew, and the early Christians needed greater clarity to define the boundaries of the faith and guard against error. In the early fourth century, controversies arose over the divinity of Jesus Christ. At the request of Emperor Constantine, Christian bishops from across the East and the West met at the town of Nicaea, near Constantinople. In AD 325 they wrote an expanded creed called the Creed of Nicaea, which they finalized in its current form at the Council of Constantinople in AD 381. Along with the Apostles' Creed, Christians widely accept the Nicene Creed as a statement of true Christian orthodoxy. As a general rule, the church employs the Apostles' Creed as the statement of faith during baptism and morning and evening Prayer, while the Nicene Creed is typically recited in services of Holy Communion.

The Athanasian Creed

The Athanasian Creed derives its name from Athanasius (293–373), an important fourth-century church leader. He is best remembered for his role as a defender of the incarnation in the conflict with Arius (and the heresy of Arianism). Arius taught that Jesus was a created being and therefore less than fully God, but at the First Council of Nicaea, Athanasius argued against this view. The matter at issue was the doctrine of *incarnation*—the belief that Jesus became truly human while remaining fully God. This was (and is) a key tenet of salvation because Jesus had to be fully God and fully human in order for his sacrificial death to atone for our sins. The Athanasian Creed was written as a statement clarifying biblical teaching and to protect the church from heresies that denied the simultaneous humanity and divinity of Jesus.

Each of these creeds is worth learning and studying in greater detail, but I offer these brief introductions here for readers who may not be familiar with them. Even though the creeds were written centuries ago, they continue to have relevance and usefulness for each new generation of Christian believers. Contrary to how they are often perceived today, the creeds are not static statements. Rather, they offer the church a range of terms, concepts, and ideas drawn from biblical teaching to address key questions of perennial importance to the church. They secure a broad unity on the essentials of our common faith. With the creeds as a foundation, we can be open to elements of diversity that continue to permeate the various church traditions. Unity in essentials gives us common ground, while our diversity provides us a means for dialogue and growth within the body of Christ. More and more people are experiencing how, with the creeds as our foundation, the church of the past can speak to the present, and the church of the present can look ahead to the future.

USING THE CREEDS IN WORSHIP

Once we recognize the importance and value of the creeds, you might wonder, *What do you do with them? Post them on the wall? Recite them in a service? Memorize them?* From the earliest times, the creeds played a significant role in the worship service as a means for Christians to affirm their common faith corporately. Today, churches across the nation are rediscovering the power of affirming their faith in the historic creeds. There are a number of ways churches are appropriating the Scriptures and the creeds into the life, worship, and ministry of their congregations.

I believe that the historic creeds belong in the worship of the church because they unite *doctrine* and *devotion*. While doctrine can often seem stuffy, boring, and useless, when it is grasped personally and the truth it conveys is treasured in the heart, it becomes surprisingly devotional. The Scriptures and the creeds help to expand our grasp of God and bring clarity to the story of our redemption. The creeds can profoundly deepen our faith as we are reminded that we, too, are a part of God's story. The more we know about the story of God, the more we love and worship him. In the words of Anglican Archbishop Michael Ramsey, "Come and pray with us, come and worship with us, and that is how you will understand what we stand for."[11]

REDISCOVERING THE LOST ART OF CATECHISM

You might think the busy streets of New York City would be one of the last places you're likely to find a renewal of Christian orthodoxy. Timothy Keller, founder of Redeemer Presbyterian Church in New York, is a *New York Times* bestselling author and a leading voice among many contemporary evangelicals in North America. His influence is felt in major cities around the world through the church planting arm of Redeemer Presbyterian, Redeemer City to City. One of the primary ways Keller has been seeking to influence the spiritual lives of Christians today is through the development of a catechism tool called the New City Catechism. This is a newly written resource aimed at helping children and adults alike learn the core doctrines of the Christian faith via fifty-two questions and answers. There is a free app for mobile devices and tablets which includes Scripture readings, prayers, and kid-friendly songs designed to help children memorize each question and answer.[12]

The New City Catechism is just one example of yet another way contemporary Christians are rediscovering the benefits of orthodoxy. Catechesis may be a foreign concept to many Christians, especially those who were not raised in a historic expression of the Christian faith, but there is a resurgence of interest in the concept, especially as a tool for discipleship. Catechesis comes from the Greek word for "instruct" or "teach"—*katecheo*. Catechesis is the process of instructing believers, both young and old, in the basics of the Christian faith. A catechism is similar to a creed but is usually structured in a question-and-answer format. Catechisms are basic summaries of the church's teachings written to ensure that all members of the church understand the essentials of the faith for themselves.

Catechism is not a new idea. Christians have used catechesis to teach the essentials of the faith for centuries. Augustine (AD 353–430), one of the church fathers, used catechesis to instruct new believers in the faith. Catechisms are not a pass-or-fail, fill-in-the-blank test, but an invitation to learn the doctrines of grace. A catechism is an invitation to a process of learning, ongoing reflection, and discussion within the community of faith, and it has been a regular and normal part of the church's discipleship for centuries. Author and theologian J. I. Packer reminds us, "Richard Baxter, John Owen, Charles Spurgeon, and countless other pastors and leaders saw catechesis as one of their most obvious and basic pastoral duties."[13]

In recent years, Packer has embarked on what he is calling his "last crusade in this world"—a call for the church to rediscover the lost art of catechesis. In their book, *Grounded in the Gospel: Building Believers the Old-Fashioned Way*, Packer and Gary Parrett explore the urgent need for the contemporary church to make catechesis an important part of its life once again. Catechesis, according to Packer and Parrett, "is the church's ministry of grounding and growing God's people in the gospel and its implications for doctrine, devotion, duty and delight."[14]

The recovery of catechesis is important for today because it provides us with an outline of the essentials of the faith through an accessible tool for training Christians, regardless of age or denominational affiliation. Many young adults feel like they have never been discipled in their faith and lack a basic understanding of Christian beliefs and spiritual practices for growing as a Christian. They see the need for catechesis and the benefits that come from using a strong, historically connected catechism. They are finding ways to incorporate this ancient form of education into their individual study, family worship, and small group gatherings. They are discovering that the simplicity of the question-and-answer format in the catechism allows them to ponder and reflect on the deep truths of Scripture in a way that forms and shapes their heads and hearts. Far from being slavishly tied to the past, the catechism helps them learn how to apply doctrine to life, an opportunity to meditate on the essentials of the Christian faith and what they might mean for following Jesus today. As they are formed and shaped by catechesis, these young Christians are experiencing holistic transformation, some for the first time.

COMPREHENSIVE WITHOUT COMPROMISE

The creeds also provide a great foundation for catechesis. This is because they offer a comprehensive understanding of the faith without compromising the core of Christianity. The creeds are beautiful because they provide boundaries, not an exhaustive list of what a person must believe on every topic. Such an approach offers balance and flexibility within an established framework, allowing tensions to exist without dividing people. This appeals to the postmodern sensibilities of young adults who want to coexist with people of different opinions while still maintaining an uncompromising core of unifying beliefs.

Over my years of teaching and pastoring, I have learned that there are inevitable tensions and paradoxes in the Christian faith, and these often lead to differences of opinion, but such differences don't need to cause division. There are uncompromising truths—the divinity of Jesus, the doctrine of the Trinity, and many others—but there are also beliefs that can accommodate a range of opinions. Since the time of the Reformation, many churches have defined themselves by what they believe in contrast to other Christians, what makes them "different" from everyone else. A new generation of young believers is far more attracted to what we have in common, emphasizing the similarities that unite us, letting those define who they are and not their differences.

Anglicanism is an example of a Christian tradition that has tried to embrace the paradoxes of the faith through the *via media*, "the middle way." One of the best examples of this is found in the life and ministry of John Wesley, who lived and died an Anglican priest. Wesley's uniquely evangelical Anglicanism is seen in his ability to find a synthesis between radical extremes and paradoxes, including the tensions between divine sovereignty and free will, evangelical and sacramental understandings of the church, and saving and sanctifying grace.[15] For the church to thrive today, we may need to borrow a page from Wesley and embrace the tension of the inherent paradoxes of the Christian faith without allowing them to tear us apart. Again, the creeds are useful in this, helping us by defining which beliefs are necessary and which ones are differences of preference. As theologian Alister McGrath has argued, Christianity at its best avoids both fundamentalism and liberalism, the first of which rejects culture and the latter of which accommodates too much to culture.[16]

There are, of course, many important issues around which the church is deeply divided. Whether these divisions are between conservatives and liberals, on the topic of human sexuality, the meaning and nature of the sacraments, or other issues, Christians can and do disagree. This is nothing new. Some of these disagreements will necessitate division, while others may allow for a measure of unity. I believe that in a world of denominational divisiveness, *comprehensiveness* can be a model. This is a concept I've borrowed from the late John Stott, who argued for "comprehensiveness without compromise." He said, "The way of separation is to pursue truth at the expense of unity. The way of compromise is to pursue unity at the expense of truth. The way of comprehension is to pursue truth and unity simultaneously, that is, to pursue the kind of unity recommended by Christ and his apostles, namely unity in truth."[17] What we need is a gracious, but comprehensive unity around orthodoxy, committed to the essentials of the historic Christian faith yet focused on loving those who disagree with us.

We must learn to speak the truth in love. The arguments and disagreements between Christian believers can often come across as unloving and, in the end, can hinder our witness to the world. We must learn to talk with those with whom we disagree. As Jesus reminds us in John 13:35, "By this all people will know that you are my disciples, if you have love for one another" (ESV). The world should know that we are followers of Jesus by our love, so if we must disagree, let us do so in a loving, Christlike way. Sometimes we must be willing to lay aside our personal and institutional biases for the sake of Christian unity and mission, learning how to live and work together to share the gospel message of Jesus Christ. Although we don't always see alike, we can agree on the essentials of the faith and join together for the common cause of Christ. The historic creeds provide a helpful lens for discerning those essentials.

Thousands of young adults like Gary and Ben, whose stories I shared at the beginning of this chapter, are finding a stability and substance for their faith around the orthodoxy articulated in the historic creeds and catechisms. They are discovering that orthodoxy is not a dry, sterile confession of the faith but rather a living affirmation of one's belief in God. What we believe influences who we are and how we live privately, but also socially and environmentally.

In the next section, we'll chart out four paths that represent how most young adults today are being drawn to liturgy. Chapter 4 will look at those who are returning to historic Christian institutions and traditions like Anglicanism, Roman Catholicism, and Eastern Orthodoxy. Chapter 5 looks at ways in which some young adults are adapting ancient monastic practices, often giving them a new twist for a contemporary context. Chapter 6 explores how some young adults are being drawn to churches that have a liturgical expression of worship, one that converges old and new. These churches, which

I have labeled "neo-liturgical," are seeking to reclaim the ancient-future roots of the faith for mission in a postmodern setting. Finally, in chapter 7 I'll introduce you to several young adults who are embracing both the charismatic tradition and liturgical worship. My hope is that these next few chapters will expose you to the diversity of this movement and showcase the variety of ways young people are utilizing and embracing the liturgical rhythms of the ancient church. Perhaps you'll resonate with one of these paths and find encouragement and practices you can incorporate along your own faith journey.

REFLECTION QUESTIONS AND PRACTICES

- How does a robust orthodox faith counteract the prevalence of Moral Therapeutic Deism (MTD)?
- Do you agree with the statement that young adults yearn for a gracious orthodoxy? Why or why not?
- Why does historic orthodox faith (as defined by the creeds) matter in an age of relativism?
- Why is the concept of "comprehensive without compromise" (focusing on the essentials, but also speaking the truth in love) an important foundation for young adults today?

PART 2

JOURNEYS

CHAPTER 4

THE APPEAL OF
THE ANCIENT
TRADITIONS

*Stand at the crossroads and look; ask for the
ancient paths, ask where the good way is, and
walk in it, and you will find rest for your souls.*

JEREMIAH 6:16

An exciting movement of young adults is gaining momentum
in Seattle, Washington. Every Sunday evening at 9:30 p.m.,
hundreds of twenty-somethings flock to St. Mark's Episcopal
Cathedral to experience the contemplative, liturgical music of the all-
male Compline Choir as they chant the ancient office of compline.
"Compline" is a Christian monastic prayer, the last prayer of each
day. It's never been considered "exciting" or seeker-friendly, and yet
these predominantly youthful crowds, many of whom won't go near a
church on Sunday morning, are present every Sunday night to listen
to this ever-ancient form of prayer, a prayer that is sung rather than
spoken. At first glance, it seems paradoxical—the younger generations are flocking to ancient rhythms and practices.

Regarding why young people attend the compline prayer service at St. Mark's and why he thinks it resonates with this crowd,

St. Mark's Dean Steve Thomason says, "It all has to do with the convergence of sacred space, sacred tradition, and the desire of people to experience the sacred and the Divine." When these young adults set foot into the cathedral and hear the choir, they immediately sense that this space is dedicated to an exclusive purpose—set apart for something beyond the ordinary, for an encounter with the divine. For many of them, it is this idea of a sacred space, a place that is distinct from the world, that offers a unique appeal. It provides them something they can't get elsewhere: a spiritual experience they don't find in most modern churches.

The example of the young adults at St. Mark's is just one illustration of the allure of liturgy, and it is not confined to neo-liturgical churches that blend ancient and modern but can also be found in far more traditional churches as well. To explore this phenomenon, I have visited dozens of traditional cathedrals and churches and have spoken with young people who have embraced the sacred traditions within these churches. The majority of these young adults are seeking liturgical expressions of worship, but they are not entering neo-liturgical churches (where ancient is mixed with contemporary worship). Instead, they are seeking out the traditional, liturgical experience. I call this group of young adults the "Cathedral and Choir" church group.

Most of these young adults are embracing one of three historic Christian traditions: Roman Catholicism, Eastern Orthodoxy, or Anglicanism. These three traditions represent the largest liturgical Christian traditions in the world. The focus of worship in these churches, for the most part, isn't about being relevant or even blending old and new. Instead, they exude a timeless aura, one not blended with our modern culture, and that characteristic is what draws these young adults to them.

For some Christians, particularly those from older generations or "low church" traditions, the liturgical traditions may be viewed with suspicion or seen as irrelevant. My purpose in this chapter is to help you better appreciate and understand the richness of the heritage these traditions offer and why young adults find them increasingly relevant today.

THE ANGLICAN TRADITION: PILGRIMS ON THE CANTERBURY TRAIL

Of the three traditions mentioned above, most of the young adults I've interviewed have embraced the Anglican church. Anglicanism traces its roots back to the time of the Roman Empire when the first Christian church came into existence on the British Isles. The term "Anglican church" arises from the Medieval Latin phrase *ecclesia anglicana* and simply means "English church." According to legend, Christianity first came to England through Joseph of Arimathea, although we can't know this for certain. What we do know is that early Christian writers mentioned the existence of a British church in the third century, and Saint Alban, who was executed in AD 209, was considered the first Christian martyr in the British Isles.[1]

Yet far from being a faith of the past, the Anglican tradition offers a refreshing alternative to postmodern uncertainty because it has a deep connection to the historic Christian faith yet speaks with relevance to our present age. Although it originated in England, Anglicanism has become one of the world's most multicultural and multiethnic churches. Anglicanism has more than seventy-million adherents in thirty-eight provinces (or regions) spread across 161 countries. The Anglican Communion is the third-largest body of Christians in the world and one of the fastest-growing in the Global South, including Asia and Africa. Located on every continent, Anglicans speak many languages and represent different races and cultures, but their love for the *Book of Common Prayer* binds them together.

To explore the allure of the Anglican tradition, I sat down for lunch with my friend Andrew Hege, a young Episcopal priest in

Lexington, Kentucky. Andrew has served as a priest for three years. He was raised in the United Church of Christ and attended several Baptist youth groups while he was growing up. During college he bounced around various non-denominational churches, never staying anywhere for long. These shifts in his spiritual development, from church to church, left him feeling disillusioned. He shared the sense of rootlessness felt by many of the young adults at the churches he attended.

All of that changed when Andrew went on a study tour in Israel during college. In Jerusalem, he experienced his first liturgical worship at St. George's Anglican Cathedral, and he describes his encounter as a "conversion to the liturgy." The powerful worship arrested him, and he had to pause to take it all in. After this encounter, he came back to the United States and began attending a small Episcopal church where the members helped him learn how to navigate his own way through the liturgy. Andrew now serves as the assistant priest at Church of the Good Shepherd, a growing congregation bustling with young adults and young families. He said their most traditional service is experiencing the most growth. Each week he sees new young faces, many of them between eighteen and thirty years old. The majority of the baptisms he performs are among young adults who are new to the tradition, a reality that is fairly uncommon for many Episcopal churches.

Andrew explained the attraction of the Anglican (Episcopal) tradition to these young adults and young families as having three drivers: mystery, beauty, and community. He believes that the sense of mystery in the church resonates for young adults because it has an allure of something distinct and different in a world that trusts primarily in the scientifically verifiable. The Anglican tradition offers an invitation to embrace transcendence and mystery, and this is expressed in the architecture, the music, and the language of the prayer book—all of which beckon young adults to come and experience something greater than themselves. "Praying the daily offices of the church roots us in the larger community of faith," he said. "The liturgy roots us in something so much larger than ourselves."

At Asbury Seminary, where I serve as the director of church planting, I met with a couple, Elizabeth Peterson and her husband, Joel. Both of them come from evangelical, non-denominational backgrounds but are drawn to Anglicanism. It was not until they returned from the mission field to Asbury in Wilmore, Kentucky, that they decided to become Anglicans. In Anglicanism, they encountered Christ in the Word and through the sacraments. The unique synergy of Roman Catholic and evangelical dimensions in worship that is found in Anglicanism is one of several factors that influenced their decision to make this tradition their spiritual home. Elizabeth describes their experience:

> On a hot, August Sunday afternoon in 2012, we walked into the service of St. Patrick's Anglican Church in Lexington, Kentucky. Thankfully we received a very clear worship guide, so we could join in the liturgy easily. We followed along and read the notes explaining why we were doing what we were doing. I managed to sit, stand, and kneel without being out of step, although it took months for me to manage to cross myself at the right time. The priest did the one thing that mattered to me more than anything else: he preached the gospel of Jesus Christ clearly, compellingly, and in a way that helped my love for Jesus to grow and assured me deeply of Christ's love for me. Since then we've been making our home in the Anglican Communion. It's a home that welcomes me as an evangelical follower of Jesus. The sermon may not be the center of the service for Anglicans, but it is central to how I grow as a disciple. Yet we've also found a home that has changed us—the thought of coming to the Lord's Table and receiving Communion only once a month or even once a year (about as often as one team we were a part of partook of the Lord's Supper) is no longer tenable for me.[2]

The Petersons' story represents thousands of other evangelicals who are embracing the Anglican tradition. As Elizabeth wrote, the formative elements of liturgy within the Anglican tradition are crucial for them.

THE ROMAN CATHOLIC CHURCH: ROME SWEET HOME

Over the past several years, stories like that of Scott and Kimberly Hahn, the authors of *Rome Sweet Home: Our Journey to Catholicism* have become more and more common. Scott and Kimberly have found a home for their faith in the Roman Catholic Church. What makes this unusual is that Scott was a Presbyterian minister— militantly anti-Catholic—until reluctantly, he began participating in the Catholic tradition. As he explored the Roman Catholic Church, he found that its faith tradition held answers to many of the questions he and Kimberly had been asking for years. Since converting to Catholicism, the couple has traveled across North America speaking about their conversion and sharing how they have found wholeness in the Roman Catholic church. Though Scott and Kimberly are Baby Boomers, their journey is similar to that of countless young adults I've met who have also found a home in the Roman Catholic Church.

The Roman Catholic Church, sometimes referred to as simply the Catholic Church, is the largest Christian church in the world, with more than 1.29 billion members worldwide. It is one of the oldest ongoing religious institutions on the planet, having played a significant role in the development of Western civilization. The Bishop of Rome, known affectionately as the Pope, stands at the center of the Roman Catholic Church's leadership and structure. The Greek word we translate as "catholic" means "universal," and it was first used to describe the church in the early second century.

Leah Libresco Sargeant represents a growing number of well-educated young adults who are finding new faith in ancient traditions such as the Catholic Church. She was raised in an atheist household on Long Island and graduated from Yale University. As a former atheist blogger, she tried to dismantle faith through her early writing. In 2012, however, she stunned her readers when she announced that she was converting to Catholicism. Since that time, Leah has appeared on CNN, and other national media outlets, to discuss her conversion from atheism to Catholicism.

In her first book, *Arriving at Amen*, Leah tells the story behind her spiritual journey, in which she encountered God through seven classic Catholic forms of prayer—Liturgy of the Hours, *Lectio Divina*, examen, intercessory prayer, the rosary, confession, and the mass. Using the rationality that defined her atheism, she examines these practices through the intellectual lens of literature, math, and art. Her journey is similar to that of many other young adults who are finding faith by returning to ancient traditions.

To understand why and how young people are being drawn to Catholicism, I visited Catholic churches to talk with priests and some of their newer young adult members. Touring the Newman Catholic Center on the campus of the University of Kentucky, I was immediately embraced by a group of university students who had just participated in prayer and confession. They were full of energy and excitement. I entered a prayer chapel and spent time praying alongside an African American student for a few minutes. After that, a friend and I took time to pose for a picture with a life-sized cardboard cutout of Pope Francis. During that campus visit, I found a diverse group of young adults all bound together by the singular tie of a shared Catholic faith. They exuded a genuine zeal for their Catholic practices.

Studies show that the "Old Mother Church" is still reaching the hearts of even the most avid postmodernists. In a recent article entitled "The Kids are Old Rite," Catholic writer Matthew Schmitz describes the surprising attraction young Catholics have to the traditional liturgy:

Step into a quiet chapel in New York and you will find an answer. There, early each Saturday morning, young worshippers gather in secret. They are divided by sex: women on the left, men on the right. Dressed in denim and Birkenstocks, with the occasional nose piercing, they could be a group of loiterers on any downtown sidewalk. But they have come here with a purpose. As a bell rings, they rise in unison. A hooded priest approaches the altar and begins to say Mass in Latin. During Communion, they kneel on the bare floor where an altar rail should be. In a city where discretion is mocked and vice goes on parade, the atmosphere of reverence is startling.[3]

Schmitz' article gives us a taste of the ethos and spirit of the Catholic worship service and hints at a few reasons why young adults are drawn to the Catholic Church. It is an ancient tradition with a deep sense of mystery and rootedness, elements that are appealing for many young people. In my own conversations with students, I sense a palpable excitement each time I meet or hear a story of someone eager to engage the well of wisdom found in church tradition.

But not all of those attracted to the ancient roots are turning to the Roman Catholic Church. Many are wary of Catholicism and have found a home not by returning to Rome but by facing east. They have found their place in the Orthodox Church.

THE ORTHODOX CHURCH: FACING EAST

With all the zeal of young evangelical Protestant missionaries, Joel and Monica travelled to Romania. Romania felt to them like an exotic and mystical land with a rich ancient heritage. It was like nothing they had ever encountered. Even though they had come to "convert the heathen," they would end up experiencing their own conversion. As Joel and Monica began building relationships with locals, a young family asked them to be godparents to their children.

The concept was foreign to them, as it is for many Western evangelicals. But this invitation introduced Joel and Monica to Romania's Orthodox Church.

Apprehensive at first, they began attending services and getting to know the people. As they did, they sensed something that had been missing in the evangelical faith of their upbringing. Could one of the world's most ancient Christian traditions have the answers they were looking for? Soon they realized the answer was a resounding "Yes!" After a great deal of prayer and soul-searching, Joel and Monica made the decision to convert to the Orthodox Church. They are now vital members of an active Orthodox parish in the United States.

The Eastern Orthodox Church is also one of the oldest and largest Christian traditions in the world, second only to Catholicism, with 225 million adherents worldwide. Sometimes it is simply referred to as the Orthodox Church, though the designation of Eastern had roots in the historical split of the Christian church into East and West. The modern Orthodox Church is a direct development of the Eastern Roman and Byzantine empires. During the early centuries of Christianity, four main providences of the ancient church emerged in the East: Antioch, Alexandria, Constantinople, and Jerusalem. In AD 324, Constantinople became the capital of the Roman Empire, and it soon became the spiritual home of the Orthodox Church. Orthodox believers base their faith and praxis on the Bible, the Seven Ecumenical Councils, the Church Fathers, the Nicene Creed, canon law, and liturgy.

To learn more about the Orthodox Church and why young people are attracted to it, I sat down with an elderly Orthodox priest named Father Daniel. Dressed in a black monk's outfit and wearing a large golden pectoral cross, he exuded humility and wisdom. From the first words of our conversation, I sensed a deep respect for the traditions of the church. Father Daniel has witnessed many young people converting to the Orthodox Church, so I asked him why he thought the Orthodox Church appeals to many young people today.

His answer was instructive: "Historical rootedness, stability of doctrine, and holiness," he said. "The Orthodox tradition is not centered in one person's ideas, like Lutheranism or Calvinism. Rather it is rooted in an ancient tradition that has not changed since the beginning." He then said, "Young people are tired of modern Christianity that focuses on self-esteem and ego. They are looking for a faith that is not diluted and is closer to the source." He ended with a smile and an encouragement: "Visit the Orthodox Church!"

I wanted to hear from younger voices as well, so I also spoke with Father Justin Patterson, an Orthodox priest for Saint Athanasius Orthodox Church, located in an unlikely place in central Kentucky. A relatively recent convert to the Orthodox Church, Father Justin began his faith journey in the Pentecostal movement. I asked him how and why he had transitioned from being a young Pentecostal to being an Eastern Orthodox priest.

Justin's answer was similar others with whom I've spoken: "I always had a nagging feeling that we (as low-church charismatics) were missing out on so much," he said. "I recall that, throughout my middle- and high-school years, I felt starved for history and a connection beyond 'the church of what's happening now.'" During college, Justin met and developed a close friendship with an Arab Orthodox Christian who traced his lineage through a Syrian Orthodox family, the direct descendants of Jews who had fled the destruction of Jerusalem in AD 70. Father Justin's friend didn't see the lineage of his faith as something extraordinary. For him, it was "no big deal—just part of the story." But Justin was fascinated by it, sensing a real connection to something old, beautiful, and wonderful. He said, "That was the beginning for me, but everything that followed in some sense flowed from this 'connection' with the ancient church that made Orthodoxy real and absolutely necessary for me."

I asked Justin to share some of the reasons why he thinks young people are joining the Orthodox Church today. He began by sharing the story of his own church:

My own parish had its roots in the early 1990s, almost a decade before its formal founding in 2002, as an outgrowth of a Bible study conducted by young people from both Asbury College and Seminary. They were on a quest, so to speak, to recover the practices of the early church. This "search for authentic Christianity" or the "faith of the early church" constituted a primary catalyst for them jumping into Orthodoxy.

Justin went on to describe Eastern Orthodoxy as far more than a belief system. For Justin, and for many young adults, Orthodoxy is a "way" of being a Christian holistically:

> I find that many people are drawn to Orthodoxy because Orthodoxy is (ironically) less a grouping of "orthodox" axioms than a way to live in fidelity to Christ. As one of my confessors once said to me: "Orthodoxy is not so much taught as it is caught." While catechesis is extremely important, you catch it by living it and experiencing it. It is a "way to live," and that way leads to Christ. Traditional liturgy for us is not about being "traditional." It is simply the "way" that Orthodox Christians worship God.

The Orthodox faith is a long and rich tradition, something that offers a direct connection to the faith of the apostles and the historic Christian church. Now that he is an Orthodox priest, Justin feels the freedom to live out his faith in the world, something he never before felt he could do with confidence.

In addition to the time I spent with Father Justin, over the past few years, I've had the opportunity to spend time with a vibrant movement among young evangelicals who have embraced the Orthodox tradition, developing significant friendships with many of them. Their stories are often the same. They were attracted to the stability and antiquity of the Orthodox tradition, and they no longer feel like they are making their own faith, but that they have joined in the "faith once delivered to the saints" (Jude 1:3). It's hard to argue with an Orthodox Christian when they tell you, "We haven't changed our worship for nearly two thousand years."

WHY YOUNG ADULTS ARE ATTRACTED TO TRADITIONAL CHURCHES

My goal in this admittedly brief survey of the three largest liturgical traditions is to give you a taste of what real people in real churches are sensing. Before we finish, I want to draw out the two common themes we find among young adults flocking to these more traditional churches.

Sacred Space

The first theme I have observed among young people is the attraction of sacred space. This includes the architecture of the church building, but it goes beyond that to the sights, smells, and symbols associated with liturgical worship in one of the historic Christian traditions. For many young people, these traditions offer "the stuff" they have been missing—tangible objects that enhance one's experience of the sacred space of worship. This can include choirs, robes, incense, candles, stained glass, historic buildings, and far more. Whereas low-church Protestant traditions focus primarily on the Word as experienced by the individual in the sermon, for traditional churches, the entire service—even the buildings and decorations—are designed to proclaim the gospel. High ceilings and ornate designs are there to help worshipers recognize that they are a part of something greater than themselves as they prepare to encounter the transcendence of Almighty God. The architecture and symbols have a defined function within the experience, bearing rich meaning and functioning in harmony with the message, prayers, songs, and words spoken to tell the story of the gospel. The physical symbols communicate this without uttering a single word. They provide a worship experience that engages the five senses.

In a recent survey, LifeWay research found that unchurched Americans prefer churches that look more like a medieval cathedral than a modern church. For the last few years, I have been on various pilgrimages to visit ancient holy sites across England to experience the atmosphere of these historic cathedrals and buildings.[4] I've visited places like Canterbury Cathedral, the birthplace of Anglicanism, and Lindisfarne Island, where famous saints like Aidan and Cuthbert evangelized northern England. These places and others like them draw millions of pilgrims every year. They exude a deep sense of spirituality and mystery and have done so for centuries. Visiting one of these "holy places" is like stepping back to the Medieval past, offering today's contemporary Christian believers a living connection to the ancient roots of their Christian faith.

Do you recall when I introduced you to St. Mark's in Seattle? Dean Steve Thomason recognized the building at St. Mark's as one of the keys for drawing youth to the Sunday night prayer. He went on to say, "It is a very unique space. Compline plays off the light and darkness theme. It is an invitation to prayer, the quietude of individual prayer."[5] In liturgical traditions, sacred space and contemplative spirituality flow together, uniting in a way that captures the heart, mind, and imagination. As we will see in a few chapters, some churches in the neo-liturgical tradition have elements of this, but those who value the aesthetics of sacred spaces tend to favor the higher church traditions like those we've seen in this chapter.

Aesthetic Beauty

Traditional, liturgical churches tend to have a long and developed approach to art, design, poetry, song, and architecture. And that's one reason why young people are flocking to these churches. Since the earliest of times, authors, poets, and artists have used their talents to depict God. Consider how many of the world's most prominent composers, artists, and musicians belong to historic Christian traditions, seeking to express the beauty they found in God through their artistic and creative gifts. The Bible itself is a work of narrative art. Narratives make up over half of Scripture as they portray how God, the great storyteller, is forming and shaping his grand narrative of redemption. But the visual arts can also tell a story by connecting with the creative imagination God has given each one of us. Throughout history, the visual arts have been one of many ways of communicating God's story, and we see examples of the power of art from the catacombs of the early church to today's modern stained-glass windows.

One reason young adults are drawn to traditional, liturgical churches is because of a renaissance among Christians emphasizing the value of the arts and a fresh appreciation for beauty and aesthetics. Some of this is happening in contrast to the pragmatic, utilitarian approach common in American churches over the past three decades. Younger generations are drawn to the arresting magnitude and beauty found in traditional churches. Just take a walk around a traditional church. You can easily find yourself caught up into another world as you soak in the beauty of iconography, stained glass, and aesthetically orchestrated music. Some of the ancient traditions, especially Orthodoxy, embrace the painting of icons as a way to employ art in worship. Deriving their name from the Greek word *eikonos* (a word denoting a likeness, profile, or figurative resemblance of an image), icons are religious paintings of Jesus Christ or one of the various saints. In some cases, they also depict biblical scenes, parables, and images from the Bible. Orthodox Christians believe icons are windows into eternity, designed to remind us of the mystery of the spiritual life we have with Christ. In the same way an icon on your computer screen opens up a new window, icons are windows that remind us that we belong to the kingdom of God. This understanding of icons is similar to the way the Celtic Christians used prayer and poetry to depict religious truths, describing what they called "thin places." A thin place is a location on earth where people come into contact with the living God. Icons and other expressions of art serve to teach and remind the worshiper of the spiritual life, as they remind us that we are part of the story of God.

While many evangelical and Protestant believers are opposed to the use of icons in worship because of concerns about idolatry, younger generations appear to be more open to them. They find that icons can be an aid to devotion by making us aware of the presence of the living God. My own personal experience with icons is an example of this. Several years ago, I went to visit my mother as she was about to undergo major surgery. I had a difficult time praying because I believed she was going to die. At the time, I was reading a book that had a picture of an icon of Christ, and whenever I saw that picture, it reminded me of his presence. Seeing it, I felt a renewed strength and courage, even when I didn't feel like praying.[6] To be clear, I wasn't praying *to* the icon, but it did serve as a visual representation of Christ and a reminder of his love for me during this time of pain and struggle.

The Anglican tradition (to which I belong) has its own artistic tradition that can be traced back to the Middle Ages and the emergence of the great English choral tradition. This beautiful tradition of vocal artistry owes its existence to the monastic movement when monks, sometimes joined by boys and lay singers, would chant the daily offices (a routine of daily prayers). Even today, cathedral choirs consisting of both adult singers and children are professionally trained and sing several times a week. Sitting in one of these beautiful choral services is like taking a step back in time, offering contemporary Christians another living connection to the history of the church. During the writing of this book, I had the privilege of sitting in the choir stall at Westminster Cathedral in London while the boys' choir sang evensong. I found it to be a powerful, ethereal experience listening to the singing of medieval hymns in a cathedral that has witnessed more than a thousand years of worship services! These examples speak to the beauty and the aesthetic appeal of liturgical traditions. Perhaps more surprising, however, is the appeal of structure and authority that these traditions offer young people today.

Structure

Historic Christian traditions also provide authority and structure, a factor that might seem unattractive when viewed in light of the dominant postmodern ethos of freedom and spontaneity. Dr. Brian Hull, professor of youth ministry at Asbury University, offers a few insights into this apparent paradox. In his view, today's young people have grown up in a world without fences or boundaries. The Baby Boomer generation emphasized individual choice and autonomy, seeking to tear down boundaries and remove restraints in order to maximize choice. Today's churches tend to be functional and utilitarian structures that resemble shopping malls more than sanctuaries. In contrast to previous generations, young adults today are rejecting this "free-for-all" and seeking out stable structures that provide a foundation for their beliefs and practices. This is one reason why they are turning to the authority and structure provided by historic church traditions.

Consider the practice of liturgical prayer, for example. Liturgical prayers were often viewed by recent generations as rote and routine, lacking in freedom to express oneself, and a barrier to authenticity and relationship. But liturgical prayers offer a structure and a backbone, something fixed and stable. Many people today will confess they don't know how to pray, when to pray, or even what to pray, and the historic prayers of the church can provide concrete help in such moments. Surprisingly, rather than feeling hindered and constrained by the structure of the liturgy, many young adults sense freedom in it. Derek, a twentysomething from Owatonna, Minnesota, makes this observation about the benefits of liturgical prayer:

> Liturgy can teach people how to pray. It can lift up the prayer lives of those who have hit a wall in praying. If people are

praying or saying what is written in a heartfelt and worshipful manner, then it has the ability to be life-changing. Granted it can simply be a "going through the motions" type of a thing, but it has the possibility to bring people together.

Another young adult named Sarah shares how the liturgy helps during her own private prayer time:

> I find the liturgical tradition attractive because it sets up a spiritual space where I can interact. This is both something I love in the mass worship context, but also in my personal prayer life as well. I love that I pray at the altar in my house. I love that I have practices of candles, icons, bowing, and journaling. All these things signify something to me, and they allow me to make spiritual space, which allows me to better commune with God and with the community of saints. Without the liturgy, I have no space—I just try to jump into Jesus without checking to see where he is.

The structure and forms of worship offered by traditional churches provide stability that many young adults are desperately seeking. As we have seen, these liturgical prayers and orders also contain powerful elements that appeal to the longings and desires of many millennials and Gen Xers, and the fixed structure is one element of this appeal. These traditional churches are offering a place of refreshment for a new generation that connects them with God through time-honored practices of the faith.

ENTERING A LITURGICAL SERVICE FOR THE FIRST TIME

For those whose Christian experience is limited to evangelical, "low-church" settings, traditional liturgy (and liturgical church services) can seem intimidating. As I shared earlier, the first time I attended a traditional Communion service, I fumbled my way through the liturgy with little idea what to do at each step during the service. For those who have not been exposed to a liturgical service, I want to offer a brief summary of the various worship postures and gestures. Why? I find that the more you know in advance, the less intimidating a service can be for those attending a liturgical church for the first time.

During a liturgical worship service, you will notice people standing, sitting, kneeling, and making various gestures at different times. Liturgical churches sometimes use this adage for understanding the postures of worship: "Kneel for prayer, stand for praise, sit for instruction." This saying acknowledges that worshiping God involves our bodies as well as our minds and emotions. Through bodily gestures, liturgical worship engages the full spectrum of human senses by employing hearing, smelling, tasting, and touching.

While these bodily actions in traditional worship services may seem intimidating at first, let me encourage you to not be intimidated or scared by them. In liturgical worship, none of the gestures are mandatory or meritorious. They are a *gift* to embrace and learn that can help you connect with God in a more tangible way as you practice them. Start by adopting the gestures that you think will aid you in your worship, and remember they are entirely optional. Another great rule of thumb for those learning liturgical practices is this: "All may, none must, some should."

Finally, know that, at their core, these practices are designed to give glory to God and assist you in worshiping him. In the next chapter, we'll learn that the attraction of the liturgy is far more than a solitary longing; it's one that is connected to our quest and desire for community.

REFLECTION QUESTIONS
AND PRACTICES

- Why does a generation that focuses so heavily the "brand-new" seem to resonate so deeply with such ancient traditions?
- Which of the three traditions listed above (Anglicanism, Roman Catholicism, and the Orthodox Church) sparked a curiosity in you?
- What is it about these sacred spaces that appeals to the senses of young adults?
- I want to challenge you to attend a liturgical service in a tradition you've never attended before. Afterward, reflect on what you experience and what emotions and thoughts it evokes in you.

CHAPTER 5

THE QUEST FOR COMMUNITY

Christian community is the place where we keep the
flame of hope alive among us and take it seriously
so that it can grow and become stronger in us.

HENRI NOUWEN

A s we continue exploring some of the more traditional expressions of liturgy, we must consider the role of monasticism in church history and the resurgence of interest in this ancient way of life today. In some pockets of Western culture, there is a renewed interest in the practice of monasticism, and it continues to be misunderstood by many people. Monasticism is an ancient tradition developed early in the life of the church by people who felt called by God to leave behind the world and live with others in solitude under a rule of faith. This "rule" was a set of practices to which they were committed that shaped their lives as individuals and as a community through the exercise of the Christian virtues of prayer, poverty, chastity, humility, and obedience.

Thomas Merton is one of the most influential contemplatives of our modern time, and his writing continues to impact the lives of millions of people worldwide. Merton, perhaps more than any other individual, has helped to bring monastic spirituality *en vogue* for many people today. After a rebellious youth, Merton converted to Roman Catholicism while attending Columbia University, and on December 10, 1941, he entered the Abbey of Our Lady of Gethsemani, a monastic community in Kentucky. His autobiography, *The Seven Storey Mountain,* chronicles his journey toward the monastic life. It has sold over one million copies with translations in over fifteen languages. Merton wrote over sixty other books as well as hundreds of poems and articles on topics ranging from contemplative prayer to the adoption of a posture of nonviolence. His writings have made him one of the most influential spiritual writers of the twentieth century.

A sixth-grade student named Susan Cahpulis once wrote to Merton, asking him for "any information whatever" that would help explain monasticism to her class. In his reply to her, he offers a helpful, user-friendly explanation of monasticism:

> The monastic life goes back a long way. Monks are people who seek to devote all their time to knowing God better and loving Him more. For that reason, they leave the cities and go out into lonely places where it is quiet and they can think. As they go on in life they want to find lonelier and lonelier places so they can think even more. In the end, people think these monks are really crazy going off by themselves and of course sometimes they are. On the other hand, when you are quiet and when you are free from a lot of cares, when you don't make enough money to pay taxes, and don't have a wife to fight with, and when your heart is quiet, you suddenly realize that everything is extremely beautiful and that just by being quiet you can almost sense that God is right there not only with you but even in you. Then you realize that it is worth the trouble of going away where you don't have to talk and mess around and make a darn fool of yourself in the middle of a lot of people who are running around in circles to no purpose. I suppose that is why monks go

off and live in lonely places . . . I suggest that you sometimes be quiet and think about how good a thing it is that you are loved by God who is infinite and who wants you to be supremely happy and who in fact is going to make you supremely happy. Isn't that something? It is, my dear, and let us keep praying that it will work out like that for everybody. Goodbye now.[1]

As we will learn in this chapter, the attraction of the monastic tradition continues to influence a new generation of young people who are learning from its rhythmic practices and embracing them for life in the twenty-first century. Similar to the neo-liturgical churches we will examine in the next chapter, there is a concerted movement of new monastic communities emerging across North America and in parts of Europe, communities that are contextualizing these ancient practices for today. At the heart of this resurgence is a longing for God expressed in and for community. In the pages that follow, I hope to introduce you to some of these communities and to some of the young people who are embracing this ancient form of spirituality for today's world.

MY ENCOUNTER AT GETHSEMANI

To experience the contemporary monastic movement firsthand, I recently spent some time on a much-needed spiritual retreat at Merton's home at Gethsemani, nestled in the rolling hills of Trappist, Kentucky. The Abbey of Gethsemani, where Merton lived for much of his adult life, is similar to other monastic centers. It is, as he called it, a "lonely place," a spiritual oasis where monks lead lives of prayer and physical labor and engage in sacred reading. Every year, thousands of people from around the world visit abbeys like this one to pray and reconnect with God.

I knew that it would not be enough to talk on the phone—I wanted to experience the monastic life for myself. So at the close of a busy season of life and ministry, I took myself to Gethsemani on a retreat to renew my spirit and to rekindle my faith. Immediately upon my arrival, I sensed this was a sacred space. Silence is tangible, felt everywhere at the abbey. All across the monastery property, signs mark areas that are "silent zones," reminding retreatants to observe silence during their time there. This fits with the spirit of monasticism, whose adherents regularly practice silence as a unique characteristic of their tradition. The sign at the entrance to the dining hall reads, "Silence is spoken here."

It was awkward and difficult at first. Imagine yourself sitting in a room full of strangers, with everyone eating together in total silence. I had to fight the urge to break the "awkwardness," and I found it to be an unusual and initially disconcerting experience that gradually turned into a calming and refreshing opportunity to rest from the noise of the world. When I eventually re-entered the world, I found myself missing those times of extended, intentional silence.

The silence of the abbey reminds those who visit how the distractions of this world can drown out the quiet voice of God within our hearts and numb us to our spiritual neediness. Silence reminds us that God is always speaking, and through many avenues, but we can easily drown out his voice with noise and activity. In the practice of stillness and solitude, God speaks to our hearts and fills us with the refreshing presence of his Spirit. In a world filled with more mental stimuli than ever, there has never been such a compelling need to rediscover the art of stillness and silence.

What does an average day look like at the abbey? Each day the monks gather one by one in silence in the sanctuary to pray the "liturgy of hours." They repeat this seven times a day, and they have a name for each time of prayer: vigils, lauds, terce, sext, none, vespers, and compline. These times make up the seven "hours" of their liturgy (also called the *Opus Dei* or "work of God"). The prayer services include a balance of singing and reciting the psalms, as well as the chanting of a hymn and other readings from Scripture. Attending one of these prayer services can feel a bit otherworldly, especially for those who have never been to one. After the first day, the daily rhythms of rest, work, and prayer that fill the monastic life tend to reorient the whole self toward the presence of God. After getting a sense of the regular routine, many who visit find themselves longing for more of these times.

As much as I enjoyed the experience, when it was over I was ready to return to "normal" life. While the time was restful and necessary, I also realized I am not cut out to be a hermit monk. Neither are most people. But the attraction of the monastic life is not just in the long-term practice of withdrawing from the world. The monastic way incorporates certain ideals and spiritual practices that can be adapted and used by anyone. At the heart of the monastic life is the Rule of St. Benedict. Benedict of Nursia lived in the sixth century and founded a community of monks at Monte Cassino, Italy. However, St. Benedict's major contribution was his "little rule for beginners," a small book that was written to serve as a foundation for community life among his monks. Benedict's Rule brought together a schedule of practices that enabled a balance of rest, work, and prayer. Benedict's Rule has since become the standard of monastic life and prayer around the world.[2]

Benedict's Rule is not just practiced by monks in monasteries; it has been read and adopted by millions of people worldwide. During my time at the abbey, I prayerfully reflected upon Benedict's rule for my own life and meditated upon its relevance for everyday life in general. The power of the Rule is that it is not just for monks, but has elements that are applicable for ordinary, everyday people. If you are not a monk, the Rule of St. Benedict has wisdom for you, too. This interest in applying the practices and values of the monastic life outside the monastery is what lies at the heart of the movement sometimes referred to as New Monasticism. New Monasticism has contextualized the rule of life that guides monastic life into various cultures and communities today, all over the world.

I have identified four different communities that serve as representative strands of the New Monasticism, though there are far more than these four. They are located in different geographical regions, and each community has different emphases and values, but together they represent yet another expression of emerging interest in ancient, liturgical practices, another way in which young adults are moving beyond the four walls of evangelical churches and into the wild world of liturgy. Let's start with a community in France.

THE TAIZÉ COMMUNITY: BURGUNDY, FRANCE

One of the neo-monastic communities famously touching the lives of thousands of young people is found in the heart of France. The Taizé Community is not your typical monastic order, and to my knowledge there is nothing like it to be found anywhere else in the world. Located in a small village in Burgundy, France, Taizé is a diverse group with members from thirty different countries and adherents from both Catholic and Protestant traditions.

The Taizé Community was founded in 1940 by Brother Roger Schütz, a Protestant from Switzerland. Brother Schütz envisioned Taizé as a place of prayer, peace, and reconciliation. In September 1940, he purchased a small house that would eventually grow into the larger Taizé Community. Brother Roger's home became a sanctuary for war refugees seeking shelter from the Nazi regime, and after the war, the community began to grow and flourish as people from all over the world joined in its vision of prayer and peace. Brother Roger once said,

> Since my youth, I think that I have never lost the intuition that community life could be a sign that God is love, and love alone. Gradually the conviction took shape in me that it was essential to create a community with [people] determined to give their whole life and who would always try to understand one another

and be reconciled, a community where kindness of heart and simplicity would be at the centre of everything.[3]

In the 1960s Taizé began to embrace youth ministry, opening its doors to younger generations. Brother Roger organized the first international young adults' meeting at Taizé in 1966, and it attracted fourteen hundred participants from thirty countries. Over the next fifty years, hundreds of thousands of young adults have visited the Taizé Community and have taken its message of peace and reconciliation back with them to their own denominations and countries of origin. Today, one of the primary missions of the Taizé Community is to bring youth together to promote reconciliation. Over one hundred thousand young people from around the world annually make pilgrimages to Taizé for prayer and worship in song, and to experience communal life together. Over the years, Taizé has been visited by major world church leaders, including several Catholic popes and archbishops of Canterbury, and most recently by the ecumenical patriarch Bartholomew, who described it as "the seat of a spiritual ecumenism, a melting-pot of reconciliation, a meeting-place that, following the extraordinary vision of Brother Roger, its founder, inspires Christians to come together."[4]

Taizé is reminiscent of the Burning Man gathering, a large gathering of young adults in Arizona each year. But it represents the longing of these young adults seeking a deeper encounter with God alongside fellow youth from around the world. In some sense, Taizé offers us a small portrait of what heaven will be like as we gather together to worship God with people from every tribe, tongue, and nation. During times of worship, hundreds and sometimes thousands of young pilgrims gather together with the monastic community there to pray, sing, and chant in many different languages. The sanctuary is filled with rich colors of deep red and gold, as well as flickering candles illuminating several dark icons. The atmosphere is one of reverence and worship. William, a young African American from New Jersey, shared his own experience at Taizé: "The repetitive chanting of the songs helps you be at peace with God and peace with yourself and quiet all the outside noise and distractions." Churches around the world have sought to incorporate their own Taizé services in their own context using Taizé CDs and sheet music, which can be found in a variety of languages.

For the past thirty years, the Taizé community has sought to spread the message of peace and reconciliation in what they call "Pilgrimages of Trust." These pilgrimages focus on crossing borders to share together in simplicity. This involves participation together in building wellsprings of trust through the beauty of shared worship and song in an effort to become people of trust and solidarity. In 2017 the Taizé community took its "Pilgrimage of Trust" to St. Louis, Missouri as a year-long initiative to reach out to the St. Louis area. Brother Alois of the Taizé community said, "As we continue the pilgrimage of trust on earth that brings together young people from many countries, we understand more and more deeply this reality: all humanity forms a single family and God lives within every human being without exception."[5]

Jason Brian Santos recently published a book titled *A Community Called Taizé: A Story of Prayer, Worship and Reconciliation*, based on his personal observations from visits to Taizé. Santos attempts to explain why young people travel from all over the world to Taizé and the impact the practices they learn there have had on their spiritual lives. Santos recognized the power of the community and wrote his PhD dissertation at Princeton Theological Seminary about the experiences of Taizé pilgrims after they leave the community and how they continue to embrace the practices they have learned there in other settings.

I had the opportunity to ask Santos about his research and what he had learned. "Young people are drawn to Taizé," Santos said, "[because] it is a Sabbath community that offers practices of silence, prayer, and community." He went on to describe what draws young adults to Taizé, saying, "Young adults are searching for something, but they are not moving *to* something, they are moving *away* from something. What the modern church of the Boomer generation has offered them doesn't satisfy their deepest longings. They want something deeper that is found in more traditional practices." Santos does not think the tradition itself attracts young people, but the depth of the *practices* that the tradition offers. In his book, Santos highlights five core practices: prayer, sacred study of Scripture, communal work, silence and solitude, and spiritual friendship. According to Santos, these five practices make up the fabric in which young adults experience Sabbath community at Taizé, together with others from around the world.

COMMUNITY OF ST. ANSELM: LONDON, ENGLAND

Another community of New Monastics can be found across the English Channel in the heart of London, England. London is home to one of the world's oldest denominations, the Church of England, and the formation of the neo-monastic community called the Community of St. Anselm began in 2015 when the Archbishop of Canterbury invited sixteen young adults ages twenty to thirty-five from around the world to spend one year in a radical, Jesus-centered community of prayer, study, and serving at Lambeth Palace in London.

According to the website for the community:

> The invitation isn't unusual—Christ calls us all to take up our cross and follow him. For these young adults, aged 20–35, this is a daring experiment in following Christ—surrendering jobs, homes, autonomy, and, in most cases, the familiarity of their own home culture and mother tongue for a year of Religious Community that draws on the ancient wisdom of St. Benedict, St. Ignatius, St. Francis, and others, and grounds it in the needs and pace of twenty-first century, cosmopolitan London.[6]

Each year, sixteen more young adults from around the world are selected to spend a year together at Lambeth Palace.

I am over the age limit for the community, but I had the honor of sitting with one of the inaugural members of the community cohort, Lindsey Runyan. I asked her what her favorite part of the experience was, and she said love for the community. "People suspect it is living in a palace in London, studying, serving the poor, traveling to monasteries, or praying the hours throughout the day. Many knew this journey for me started with a passion kindled by exploring the ancient traditions of the church and monasticism. However, my answer is always the same; my favorite part was the people."

Lindsey went on to explain that it was the *diversity* of the community that was the most significant part of the experience for her:

> We were sixteen very different people from all around the world, and we came from distinctive church traditions, careers, and educational backgrounds. I lived with French Roman Catholics, Kenyan Pentecostals, Baptists, Free Methodists, and people representing the spectrum of the Anglican Communion from Australia, Kenya, England, Belgium, and the United States. We did not make tea the same way, fought about how to clean a bathroom properly and whether a sport was called football or soccer. Our expressions of worship and ideas of community were completely different, but we came together and worshipped one God together in one Spirit. We were united in Christ. We were young adults from all around the world coming from different denominations, hungry to seek more of God in our lives, and being set apart to drop everything we knew to live a life in community. We did not always get along or empathize with each other or understand one another's worship styles, but that is what a community is, what a family is, growing and learning from each other, living

as the body of Christ. Our foundation is in Jesus Christ alone. The aspects of our denominations were the things that made us unique rather than divided us.

According to Lindsey, the most impactful moments were the small, ordinary times God used to transform her. She said,

> Washing dishes together, playing sports, learning an African dance in the kitchen, praying with one another, partaking in the Eucharist each day, having struggles and knowing that I did not have to do this alone were the places I saw God working slowly and deeply in my life. Community, for me, is a place not measured in success like the world, but a place to belong and for me to be myself.

Lindsey's account of her time in the Community of St. Anselm confirms a universal hunger for unity and community transcending denomination, gender, and cultural background.

For resident member Rachael Lopez, it was her discovery of the convergence of ancient and new paths of prayer that surprised her most about her time at the Community of St. Anselm. She reflected back on her study of photography and the analogy to the practice of prayer: "When I studied photography, I loved using both old and new processes. I made digital negatives from film stills and created cyanotypes, a chemical process discovered in the 1840s. The pieces needed a few hours of direct sunlight, so I spent several days in the middle of winter walking around Melbourne, chasing the sun. I was inspired by Lewis Hyde, who wrote, 'A live tradition extends in both directions in time.' While he was referring to artists, I believe it applies to the church as well. In my time with the Community of St. Anselm, I have discovered it is possible to have a genuine love of prayers and songs in all their forms—old and new, liturgical and spontaneous. I have seen this work together beautifully."[7]

The Community of St. Anselm gives us a wonderful picture of how life lived together often proves to be a transformative experience. Both Rachael's and Lindsay's experiences speak to the power of communal living when it is structured according to the ancient rhythms of the church.

THE SIMPLE WAY:
PHILADELPHIA, PENNSYLVANIA

Another well-known example of New Monasticism can be found in the inner city of Philadelphia, Pennsylvania, in the United States at a monastic community called The Simple Way. In 1995, Shane Claiborne and a small group of friends founded The Simple Way as an intentional community living together on mission. Claiborne is a social activist and the author of *The Irresistible Revolution: Living as an Ordinary Radical.* Together, he and the other founders set out to settle in the poorest area of the city with a vision for cultivating an apostolic Christian community. The Simple Way's website states, "We have been inspired by the early church in the book of Acts, where the Bible says the early Christians shared all their possessions in common, gave freely to those in need, and met in each other's homes for worship. The Gospel was lived out of dinner tables and living rooms. And now—after over two decades—an intentional community has turned into a little village."[8]

The Simple Way is made up of three groups of people: the "remainers" (long-term, indigenous residents), the "returners" (people from the neighborhood who have come back to be a part of the restoration), and the "relocators" (non-indigenous friends who have moved here to intentionally bring their gifts and energy). Members of The Simple Way participate in city transformation through a variety of social justice outreaches including community gardens, running a store, and feeding the hungry. They describe their work in the following way: "We have a cluster of about a dozen properties on the same block—houses and gardens we share. We are building a park and a green space where a fire burned down part of our neighborhood in 2007. We paint murals, help kids with homework, share food, host neighborhood celebrations, and try to live as one big family . . . which means eating together, praying together, doing life together."[9]

Claiborne and Jonathan Wilson-Hartgrove are two of the most visible leaders of the New Monasticism movement in the United States. Wilson-Hartgrove is the founder of Rutba House, a community of hospitality in the historic neighborhood of Walltown in Philadelphia. Along with several other new monastic leaders, they drafted the following twelve marks as a formal summary of the new monasticism, marks detailed further in the book *School(s) for Conversion: 12 Marks of a New Monasticism*. Here are the twelve marks, along with the context behind them:

> Moved by God's Spirit in this time called America to assemble at St. Johns Baptist Church in Durham, N.C., we wish to acknowledge a movement of radical rebirth, grounded in God's love and drawing on the rich tradition of Christian practices that have long formed disciples in the simple Way of Christ. This contemporary school for conversion which we have called a "new monasticism" is producing a grassroots ecumenism and a prophetic witness within the North American church which is diverse in form but characterized by the following marks:
>
> 1. Relocation to the abandoned places of Empire.
> 2. Sharing economic resources with fellow community members and the needy among us.
> 3. Hospitality to the stranger.
> 4. Lament for racial divisions within the church and our communities combined with the active pursuit of a just reconciliation.
> 5. Humble submission to Christ's body, the church.

6. Intentional formation in the way of Christ and the rule of the community along the lines of the old novitiate.

7. Nurturing common life among members of intentional community.

8. Support for celibate singles alongside monogamous married couples and their children.

9. Geographical proximity to community members who share a common rule of life.

10. Care for the plot of God's earth given to us along with support of our local economies.

11. Peacemaking in the midst of violence and conflict resolution within communities along the lines of Matthew 18.

12. Commitment to a disciplined contemplative life.[10]

These twelve practices draw upon some of the historic monastic practices but frame them in a new, contemporary context. Just as the monastics of old sought to live in intentional community in a specific geographic location, joining together in prayer and common life, New Monasticism is doing this in a twenty-first century context. These marks give us some additional clues to help us better understand how and why young adults today are drawn to the liturgical, ancient rhythms of Christianity, particularly the attraction of a distinct form of communal life together.

THE SPIRITUAL FRIENDSHIP MOVEMENT

A fourth and final example of how young adults are drawing from the monastic tradition is a movement centered around the concept of "spiritual friendship." Unlike the other movements I've mentioned, this is not a geographically defined movement, but it's still a strong community. What unites today's young adults who adhere to the spiritual friendship movement is a commitment to living a single, celibate lifestyle. Many of the leaders of this movement are also gay yet committed to celibacy.

The spiritual friendship movement draws from the ancient monastic tradition in an attempt to recover the value of committed relationships through vows and covenantal agreements between individuals. God made us to live in community with others, and as the monk and reformer Martin Luther once said, "God has created man for fellowship, and not for solitariness."[11] The movement draws deeply from the monastic tradition and from figures like Aelred (1110-1167), the English Cistercian monk and Abbot of Rievaulx in North Yorkshire, England, from 1147 until his death. Aelred is perhaps best known for his works *On Spiritual Friendship* and *The Mirror of Charity*, and he has become the patron saint of friendship. Aelred once famously said, "See to what limits love should reach among friends, namely to a willingness to die for each other."[12]

With its unique focus on reclaiming the historic teaching on celibacy, the value of the single life, and the need for deep spiritual friendships, this movement offers a counter-cultural perspective on one of the major cultural challenges facing the church today: human sexuality. Many of the leading voices of this movement are young, gay, celibate Christians, and most have found a home in the liturgical traditions of the church. Leading advocates include Wesley Hill, an Anglican professor near Pittsburgh; Eve Tushnet, a Catholic who writes from Washington, DC; and Gregg Webb, an Eastern Orthodox believer studying at Covenant Theological Seminary in St. Louis, Missouri. Wesley Hill may be the most well-known voice among the group, as his book *Spiritual Friendship: Finding Love in the Church as a Celibate Gay Christian* has received national acclaim. Wesley defines friendship as "a good and godly love in its own right, just as worthy of attention, nurture, and respect as any other form of Christian affection. That's what the Christian tradition has mainly said. And that's what I want to say—frrom a fresh angle of vision—in this book, too."[13]

I had the opportunity to talk with Wesley about his book, its impact, and the connections to the monastic movement of the past. I began by asking him if he believes spiritual friendship is a form of monasticism. He responded by pointing out the parallels between the rediscovery of intimacy and friendship. However, he continued, admitting that the movement was still young, "We have been wrestling with [the question], what does [spiritual friendship] look like practically? In many ways, the new monastic movement is ahead of us. We haven't developed an official rule of life or way to do this. I am often asked, 'How do I live this out?'" Hill said one of the challenges of the spiritual friendship movement is that it is still emerging. It's a living experiment. Some adherents are in intentional living arrangements with families, others are living in shared housing, while still others are exploring other ways of living out the values of spiritual friendship in their own contexts.

I was particularly intrigued by the connections between the spiritual friendship movement and the historic liturgical traditions of the church. I asked Wesley about this, and he agreed, saying, "Anglican and Catholic traditions have had a long history of intentionally thinking through celibacy. For them it's not just singles ministry. When I was first trying to live as a gay celibate Christian, I wanted to know where I could do that. Anglicans and those from thick liturgical traditions have thought about intentional celibacy. A lot of people have found a refuge in Anglicanism because it is a generous place. It's a big tent. It actually has things to say about the celibate life." Again, we find young adults drawn to the wisdom and the long history of reflection and practice in the liturgical tradition. They find a substantial foundation for addressing some of the culture's most pressing questions.

LESSONS FROM NEW MONASTICISM

What, if anything, can we learn from these examples of new monastic communities? What can they teach us? First, we should note that the New Monasticism as a movement draws its inspiration from the ancient monastic traditions, yet it is not identical to them. It seeks to embody the tenets of monasticism in response to the contexts we face today and the challenges of the twenty-first century. Times change and contexts change, and this new movement isn't looking to simply withdraw from the world, but to draw from ancient practices and time-honored principles in order to address today's problems. This simple principle of blending the old and new can be seen in the movement's forms of prayer and liturgy, and it reminds us that the interest of young adults includes an aspect of appropriation. Young adults are intrigued by the past, but often as a well from which to draw upon, reaching into the from various streams of church tradition in order to renew our faith today. New Monasticism can provide a model for the future of the church, one that is rooted in the past but also engages present culture with a faith that is ever ancient, ever new.

Yet another lesson we can draw from these movements is the strong emphasis they place on community life. Churches led by those of the Baby Boomer generation are often structured around the needs and desires of individuals. Young adults today are interested in community, and they appreciate the connection to ancient communities like the monastics. Again, this interest is expressed and lived out in a variety of different ways. For some, this might literally mean living together in a form of commune, while for others it might involve intentionally setting aside time to invest in deeper, covenantal friendships. Common life together is at the heart of identity as members of the body of Christ. Monasticism reminds us that we share a common life, a common call, and a common responsibility to love and serve one another.

For many of these young adults, living out their faith in this way is most like a secular monastic order, where men and women live out their faith with a shared rule of life in the world outside the walls of a monastery. Although they may live in different parts of the world, they have a common commitment to a way of life that is called "a rule of life." A rule of life can help individuals commit themselves to daily spiritual practices that enable them to grow in faith. A rule of life is not a law that binds; it functions simply as a guide to regulate one's spiritual life. In recent years, I have seen a growing number of young people embrace a common rule of life as they covenant together with others to grow on their spiritual journey.

Another lesson we can learn from these new monastic communities is a commitment to reconciliation and unity among Christians, especially among the various traditions of the church. Many of these communal expressions are ecumenically minded and are committed to the unity of all Christians. These new monastic communities remind us that there is unity *as well as diversity* in the body of Christ. They have rediscovered Jesus' prayer that we may all be one (John 17), and their shared lives provides a model for how Christians can practice fellowship across the great traditions of the Christian church. Oftentimes, the communities themselves are interdenominational and are open to learning from people of other denominations and nationalities. This type of unity through diversity helps us see Christianity as a large family with a unique dynamism, a family that can speak to generations to come with an open embrace of others who may not look, think, or act like we do.

A final lesson we can learn from the new monastic movement is the urgent need to recover biblical hospitality. At the heart of Benedict's Rule is the practice of hospitality, and this is one of the reasons why monasteries open their doors to thousands of strangers every year. Sadly, many contemporary Christians and churches have lost touch with the biblical importance of extending hospitality to strangers. The word hospitality literally means "love of strangers," and it is found several times in the New Testament (Rom. 12:13; 1 Tim. 3:2; Titus 1:8; 1 Pet. 4:9). St. Benedict, in his rule of life, reminds us, in a paraphrase of Matthew 25:35: "Let all guests who arrive be received like Christ, for he is going to say, 'I came as a guest, and you received me.'" We are all called to offer the love of Christ to our guests and welcome them in such a way that our evident love and actions toward them will help to change them from strangers into friends.

While many traditional monasteries are, sadly, on the verge of closing today, it is my hope that young adults who have been influenced by the rich monastic tradition will carry on the monastic legacy through the sacred rhythms of love, work, and prayer. Rob Dreher, in his controversial book *The Benedict Option,* has suggested that the future of Christianity in the West will happen through a recovery of monastic ideals.[14] Perhaps this will happen through these younger Christians who have embraced the ideals of monastic life. The recovery of monastic wisdom and spirituality as way of life can offer the church a foundation to preserve it through the changes and challenges that lie ahead. After all, if something has lasted for over 1,500 years, who are we to say it can't last another thousand?

REFLECTION QUESTIONS AND PRACTICES

- What do you think is driving the resurgence of interest in monastic principles?
- Throughout the chapter, we looked at several neo-monastic communities around the world. Which one of these did you find most intriguing? Why?
- The scarlet thread that runs through this chapter is the quest for community. What similarities do you see in the different stories and expressions of community? What are the differences?
- If you have never experienced a retreat at a monastery, I invite you to find one near you and take a day to experience what it is like to live so distant from the busyness of life in a holy community. Be sure to reflect on the difficulties as well as the refreshing qualities of entering such a community.

CHAPTER 6

SOMETHING ANCIENT, SOMETHING NEW

*Therefore every teacher of the law who has
become a disciple in the kingdom of heaven is
like the owner of a house who brings out of his
storeroom new treasures as well as old.*

JESUS (MATT. 13:52)

Several years ago my family and I travelled to Raleigh, North Carolina, hoping to avoid a hurricane. My friend, Tony Merida, is the pastor of Imago Dei Church and a preaching professor as Southeastern Baptist Theological Seminary, and he had invited us to attend his new church. From the moment we arrived, we realized that Imago Dei was not your typical Baptist church plant. For starters, we noticed that it was buzzing with twenty- and thirty-somethings, many of whom were seminary or university students. As we experienced worship with them, I was surprised to see them reclaiming several elements of historical liturgy. Imago Dei is one of many churches today that represents a growing trend among young adults: joining the ancient with the new.

Imago Dei is also different from other Baptist churches in celebrating the Lord's Supper every Sunday and reciting the historic creeds of the faith. Here is how they describe their worship:

Certain aspects of the service will be consistent every week. One of those aspects is reading Scripture out loud together. At times, we also recite ancient confessions like The Apostle's Creed, and we often conclude by reciting a biblical prayer, such as the Lord's Prayer.

You can expect a mix of modern and ancient songs that magnify Christ. Our worship leader strives to lead us in songs that are biblically faithful and full of praise to God.

We take the Lord's Supper every Sunday in order to remember Christ's atoning death and our identity as members of one body. This is also a time for repentance and renewal.[1]

While this combination of practices is atypical for Baptist churches, Imago Dei is not alone. It's been on a journey with hundreds of other churches from various denominational backgrounds that are reclaiming the historic forms of worship and appropriating them for contemporary contexts. These churches are not just adopting the ancient practices, they are often contextualizing them or changing them in subtle ways to incorporate them within the context of a modern worship experience. I refer to these churches as "neo-liturgical churches," and they make up a distinct movement that is experimenting with new forms of liturgical worship, blending old with new. By utilizing both historic and modern aspects of worship, neo-liturgical churches are resonating deeply with many young adults.

As we've seen, the historic traditions of the Christian church— Roman Catholic, Anglican, and Eastern Orthodox—have developed liturgies rooted in long-standing practices and traditions. These are sometimes called the "high church" traditions, and as we saw earlier, they are attracting many young adults who appreciate their stability and longevity. There are also some young believers who are emerging from less traditional churches, yet who are not ready to leave behind their church experience for a traditional one. Instead of making it *either* ancient or new, they are trying to have both.

This convergence of old and new resonates deeply with many young adults I've interviewed. While neo-liturgical churches offer a sense of historical rootedness and cultivating a culture of belonging, they also continue to find culturally relevant points of connection, including a modern worship experience that incorporates contemporary instruments and worship songs. This enables the church to tap into the allure young adults feel toward the liturgical tradition while avoiding the stigma of being viewed as dry, boring, and outdated. Obviously, there is a tension here, as we must avoid inappropriate appropriation by cherry-picking customs here and there from the liturgy without an understanding of the context in which they were created.

The purpose of this chapter is to show how the blending of liturgical worship in a modern context is a popular and successful way of meeting the needs of young adults today. These churches do this by connecting history with the present. In the pages that follow, I want to introduce you to several neo-liturgical churches so you can hear from them firsthand and learn how they are recovering ancient practices in the context of a modern service. While there are countless examples to draw from, I selected these churches because they represent a diversity of styles and traditions within this movement.

OFFERINGS COMMUNITY OF FIRST UMC: LEXINGTON, KENTUCKY

In the heart of Lexington, Kentucky, Offerings Community of First United Methodist Church represents a congregation of young adults who embrace what some are calling "convergent" worship. Teddy Ray, lead pastor of Offerings, has seen the value of rooting his church in the historical practices of Word and table while also maintaining a contemporary aspect to the service. Teddy is a Methodist minister who started Offerings Community as a contemporary youth worship service of First United Methodist Church in Lexington with only a handful of youth and young adults. Over the last few years, they have grown into an inter-generational community of young adults, families, and children. As the church has developed its own distinct identity over the years, it has transitioned into a neo-liturgical fellowship. Through the years, the Offerings team has learned to contextualize the historic practices of the church for today's Christian, including the style, design, and architecture of the worship space. For example, their worship space portrays the images of many ancient icons.

The bridging of the gap between ancient and modern begins with a reorientation of how worship experiences are defined. When I asked whether Offerings conducts a contemporary or traditional worship service, Teddy responded by sharing a paradigm shift they've made. He said he'd like to change the conversation regarding Offerings' style of worship, so when people ask him that question, he tells them, "We do *Word* and *table* worship." Of course, people aren't used to descriptions of worship formulated around the substance of the service as opposed to the style of music played. Teddy said, however, "This is the best description I can give. In fact, it's the only description I can give and know it will remain true. Every week, we hear the Word of God. Week after week it comes to us to guide, rebuke, encourage, or correct. And every week, we come to the Lord's Table to commemorate Christ's sacrificial death, participate in his body and blood, and receive the spiritual strengthening to do his will. Word and table—*these* are the essentials of our worship, and nothing else."

This form of worship has created expectations among the worshipers, but these are based upon substance rather than style.

What's the takeaway here? For Offerings, worship is not about style. Rather, it is about recovering the content and substance within a liturgical tradition for a postmodern context through the Word and table structure.

SOJOURN COMMUNITY CHURCH: LOUISVILLE, KENTUCKY

Yet another example of a fresh expression of liturgical innovation is Sojourn Community Church, located in the heart of Louisville, Kentucky. Sojourn draws a large number of young adults from Southern Seminary, the flagship seminary of the Southern Baptist Convention. Like Imago Dei, highlighted earlier, this is not your typical Baptist church. Mike Cosper, pastor of worship and arts, describes Sojourn's liturgical journey:

> At Sojourn, we came to embrace a loosely liturgical model about seven years ago. The decision came not out of a desire to reform our worship services, but out of a broader desire to root everything we do in the gospel. As we dialogued about worship, we came to see that the historic rhythms of liturgical worship helped to reinforce and remember the rhythms of the gospel.

Sojourn is a good example of what is referred to as "liturgical catechesis." As we saw earlier, catechesis is a way of teaching using repetition and a question-and-answer format. Liturgical catechesis teaches the faith through the repetition of words, prayers, and songs that are sung each week. At Sojourn, the addition of formal liturgy helped create rhythms that led people to embrace a more gospel-centered worship. Cosper describes the pattern of their liturgy through four general movements: Adoration (God is holy), confession and lament (we are sinners), assurance (Jesus saves us from our sin), and sending (the Holy Spirit sends us on mission). In an interview for The Gospel Coalition's website, Cosper said,

> Within these broad categories are weekly practices, including a call to worship, confession of sin, passing the peace, and so on. Each service comes to a climax at the Communion table and ends

with a sense of commitment and commission. It's like "gospel practice"—a rehearsal of the rhythms of the gospel that not only mark conversion, but mark the everyday life of Christians.[2]

Sojourn has carefully crafted a theologically robust liturgy, and they help teach the gospel to their members in a way that is memorable and lasting.

PANGEA CHURCH: SEATTLE, WASHINGTON

One last example of a neo-liturgical church I want to share with you is found in the heart of Seattle, Washington, one of the most unchurched cities in the nation. In 2010, Kurt and Linda Willem moved from California to Seattle to start Pangea Church in partnership with the Brethren in Christ. Liturgy isn't the first thing that comes to mind when most people think of the Anabaptist tradition to which the Brethren belong. The name of the church is derived from the Greek word *pangea*, which means "entire earth." Kurt Willem's dream, as he shared, "is that Pangea will become a church that stands up for the oppressed, empowers families, includes the excluded, cultivates friendship, ignites activism, and creates space for exploring spirituality."[3]

At first, Pangea Church looks like your typical evangelical church in America. But a closer look reveals an unusual convergence of traditions. Though they are Anabaptist (a low church tradition that eschews liturgical practices), they have partnered with St. Luke's Episcopal Church, where they meet for worship. The Anabaptist values show through in their identity as a "peace church," one that believes in non-violence, but they also draw from a wide variety of other traditions. Kurt said,

[We have adopted practices from] progressive forms of evangelicalism (not the sort on the news!): Eastern Orthodoxy, Roman Catholicism, Anglicanism (lots of influence!), Wesleyanism, the missional church, emerging church, and so many more. We have a strong commitment to ecumenical relationships (to our theological left and right) and see ourselves in fidelity with all Christians who rally around the centrality of the bodily resurrection of Christ, along with the basic beliefs expressed by the Apostles' Creed (whether or not they consider themselves "creedal").

Pangea shares many of the common marks of other neo-liturgical churches that value and practice liturgical worship. They describe their worship as a blend of ancient and modern influences, using video and a live worship music band. Sermons are taught in series that connect with the realities of everyday life, while the liturgy incorporates ancient forms of worship with an emphasis on celebrating the Eucharist. On their website they list some of the practices shaped by their ancient-future impulse, including:

- Liturgical readings within worship.
- An embrace of the "real presence" of Christ within the Holy Communion (not to be confused with the Roman Catholic doctrine of transubstantiation). The Eucharist is a means of grace through which the Holy Spirit empowers us as community to join God's mission in our neighborhoods, workplaces, families, city, and world. Therefore, we take the elements every Sunday. This is perhaps our one major departure from historical Anabaptist practice and theology.
- Situating worship within the Christian Calendar: Advent, Christmas, Epiphany, Lent, Holy Week, Easter, and Pentecost.
- Bodily prayer such as kneeling and the sign of the cross.[4]

Pangea is a unique church, an eclectic mix of old and new that draws inspiration from several different traditions and denominations. Their worship is a blend of contemporary and ancient where younger adults feel at home in a casual and laid-back atmosphere.

Some have questioned if it is possible to combine all of this in one worship service. If you have doubts, I invite you to visit Seattle and experience Pangea to see firsthand how they are bridging these disparate worlds into a single service of worship.

WHY DO NEO-LITURGICAL CHURCHES RESONATE SO STRONGLY WITH PEOPLE?

These examples of churches highlight how the embrace of neo-liturgical worship—an eclectic combination of old and new forms of liturgy—is taking hold in many congregations all across the theological and denominational spectrum. While each church is unique, these congregations share something in common: a creative balance of historic liturgy and contemporary elements of modern worship. Each of these neo-liturgical churches are also attracting many millennials and Gen Xers. Because of this, they offer us additional insight into the reasons why young adults feel drawn to liturgical worship.

In a previous chapter, I looked at some of the reasons why young adults are attracted to historical expressions of liturgical worship. But here I want to describe what *neo-liturgical churches in particular* offer that is alluring to this new generation. What is it about neo-liturgical churches and the way they worship that resonates with young adults?

Ancient and Modern Worship

For most evangelical Americans, worship is immediately equated with music—with a specific style of music. But as we noted earlier, this understanding of worship is far too limiting. It's not biblical, and it leads to a reduction in our understanding of the rich history and development of worship over the centuries. Worship is singing, but it is more. It is the act of giving all of ourselves back to God by giving him respect, reverence, honor, and glory. God is worthy of our highest praise and worship, and he has called us to live all of life "to the praise of his glory" (Eph. 1:12). True worship of God begins in our hearts as we give adoration, glory, and praise to God, and it manifests itself outwardly as we lift up our voices to God in prayer, praise, and song. But it's not enough to simply know and mentally comprehend the definition of worship. We, as living beings, must practice worship, and liturgy offers us a tangible and interactive structure in which worship can freely occur.

For many young adults, the embrace of liturgy leads to greater freedom in worship. Many young adults feel at home in neo-liturgical churches because of the blend of the ancient and modern. Susan, who is in her twenties, told me, "Our worship is both formal and informal, so we can come as we are yet feel a part of something bigger than us. Through the liturgy, we don't have to worry about what's coming next. The words and prayers of the liturgy that we say each week sink deep into our hearts and allow us to worship from the heart." The ancient-modern vibe meets two longings: a desire to connect with friends in a shared faith experience, and a connection to the past, sort of like a reunion with family members who bring wisdom, maturity, and perspective.

Neo-liturgical worship services often feel very intimate, akin to worshiping in a living room. Some neo-liturgical churches even design their worship space to reflect this aesthetic of intimacy by using candles, icons, tapestries, and congregational seating that is circular rather than linear. Many churches write their own songs and prayers to embody the embrace of both old and new. Written prayers are one way neo-liturgical churches involve the entire church body in worship, by allowing various members to come forward and offer prayer on behalf of the community of faith. Many churches also have prayer stations, crosses, and designated places in the sanctuary where people receive prayer during the service.

Word and Table

Earlier, when we looked at Offerings Community, they used the term "word and table" to describe their worship. But this way of framing worship is not unique to Offerings. It is a popular way of structuring the liturgy and worship in a neo-liturgical church today, a model of worship in which the Word refers to the place of Scripture reading, teaching, and preaching of the Word of God in the worship service, while the reference to the table refers to the Lord's Supper, the act of remembering the death of Jesus Christ and anticipating his second coming by partaking of bread and wine.[5]

Word and table structure isn't a static form of worship, rather it provides a framework that these churches are building upon. Many of these churches are infusing their liturgical worship with contemporary forms of artistic expression that connect with the hearts and minds of young adults today. Every week, neo-liturgical churches retell the gospel story through the structure of their liturgy while utilizing additional contemporary connection points: modern music styles, paintings, and other art forms in conjunction with the Word and table.

Sense of Community

One of the first things people notice when they step into a neo-liturgical church is the warm environment and strong sense of community among the members. Almost universally you will find a coffee station in the lobby, with young people gathered around drinking lattes and talking about life together. A common joke is that coffee is another sacrament in these churches, one that prepares people for worship. This intentional cultivation of community goes beyond a service or experience of corporate worship, as most of these churches place a strong emphasis on small groups, gathering together throughout the week across the cities to meet in homes, bars, or coffee houses.

Many of the leaders I met were humble about their churches and radiated a strong sense of authenticity. In several cases, it was difficult to differentiate the leaders from the members until people separated from the group to lead worship or preach the sermon.

The leaders blend in with the people, as one of the community. Leaders in neo-liturgical churches place a strong emphasis on being accessible, "just one of the members of the church." One member told me, "Our pastor is just like one of us. On Sundays, you don't know who the pastor is until he gets up to preach."

Socially and Missionally Minded

For many neo-liturgical churches, the work of worship continues long beyond the Sunday service. Most of the churches I encountered were also deeply committed to social justice issues and had a strong focus on outreach. This resonates with young people who want to make a difference in the world, who don't just want to send money to feed the homeless. They want to get their hands dirty and invest themselves personally in helping and serving people.

There are millions of people living in poverty in the United States, despite the overall wealth of our nation. Hunger and poverty are becoming a serious epidemic, and most of our nation's poor are children and the elderly. Neo-liturgical churches are engaging the poor, seeking to serve these communities, and living out an embodied spirituality that engages the world around them on a practical, tangible level—not just an emotional or inwardly spiritual level.

MY JOURNEY INTO NEO-LITURGICAL WORSHIP

As someone who has been on his own liturgical journey from a "low church" background to the Anglican church, I found much in the neo-liturgical movement that resonated with me. In particular, I found myself drawn to the balance of Word and table, and to the embrace of simultaneous ancient and modern worship. In 2005, my wife and I planted a non-denominational church with nothing but some faith and the clothes on our backs. The church began meeting in a home with five people, and in the first few years it grew to several hundred people from all ages and backgrounds, including many younger people from the surfing community on the East Coast.

We began with a very contemporary worship style, meeting in a YMCA gym with stage lighting and loud music and good, strong coffee. At one point, we were known as the "surfer church," but as time passed we sensed a growing hunger for something more than the contemporary and cool. We longed for greater substance and stability, and we began to look to church history for wisdom, drawing on the classic Christian liturgical tradition. In 2010, I wrote a book-length introduction to the Apostles' Creed called *Creed: Connect to the Historic Essentials of the Faith* to introduce our young people to the historic roots of the faith. It eventually led us into a deeper search of recovering traditional forms of worship.

We did not stop there. In addition to studying church tradition, we began to incorporate several liturgical practices into our worship. Around this time, two retired priests joined our church and helped us transition to a neo-liturgical church, bringing together the best of church tradition with contemporary worship in a way that connected with the hearts and minds of congregants, both young and old. When anyone asked how us how we would describe our church, we said it was a "fresh expression of an ancient faith." Eventually, we became one church with two expressions and two Sunday worship services: a traditional liturgical service with robes and colored vestments, and a contemporary blended service. Each service featured aspects of historic liturgical worship that included the reading of Scripture, the celebration of the Eucharist, and the reciting of the Lord's Prayer. On Sunday mornings people found a welcoming, family-friendly atmosphere *and* a unique worship experience where they met with God. We didn't plan to become a neo-liturgical church, but along the way found we were led to embrace the historic roots of the Christian faith.

As we have seen in this chapter, neo-liturgical churches are not unique to a particular person or church denomination. Many of these churches have come to embrace the richness of the liturgical way of living out the Christian faith after a period of searching, out of a longing for deeper roots and a connection to the past. Young adults are often attracted to these churches because they combine the best of both worlds, providing spiritual formation practices that are rooted in the Christian tradition along with an emphasis on deep community with others. As I've walked this path in my own life, I have met countless others who are longing for a faith with deep roots in history and tradition, not driven by fads.

Yet as popular as neo-liturgical churches are, they aren't the only places we see young adults embracing liturgy. In the next chapter, we'll look at another type of "blended" church, one that has developed from the charismatic movement, seeking to combine openness to the Holy Spirit with the structures of historic, liturgical worship. My hope is that as you are introduced to each of the various expressions of this embrace of liturgy, you will discover a new appreciation—perhaps even a longing in your own heart—for these expressions of worship. As we will see in the next chapter, the Holy Spirit is not opposed to the structures of liturgy. The Spirit is always active in the church, and in many cases, the structures of the ancient church can provide a welcome connection to the ways God has moved in the past, inviting revival for today and hope for the future.

REFLECTION QUESTIONS AND PRACTICES

- The churches we explored in this chapter are implementing a convergence of old and new. What do you think about this convergence and its potential impact on the future of the church?
- What common themes do you see within these churches? Why are they impactful?
- Do you see this movement as a passing trend/fad, or is there something much deeper going on? Why?
- I want to challenge you to seek out a neo-liturgical church near you and visit as you are able. Afterward, reflect on what you experience and the emotions and thoughts it evokes in you.

CHAPTER 7

THREE STREAMS, ONE RIVER

A great new convergence of the traditions
are occurring which will change the face of
the church in the next hundred years.
RICHARD LOVELACE

A few years ago, my friend Kris McDaniel and a few of his closest friends planted a church through the Vineyard Movement to reach their friends in downtown Atlanta, Georgia. Over the course of several years, this church plant became an Anglican church, one that embraces evangelical and liturgical dimensions of the Christian faith, yet also retains an emphasis on the present-day gifts of the Spirit. Today, Trinity Anglican Mission has over one thousand members on two campuses, and a majority of the members are young adults under the age of thirty-five.

After learning of their story and their embrace of liturgy, I called Kris and spoke with him about their journey from the Vineyard Movement to the Anglican Church. Kris suggested I fly out to Atlanta to see for myself what the Lord was doing at Trinity, so I accepted his offer and booked a plane ticket. Not knowing what I was getting into, I boarded a plane to spend a weekend observing the church and listening to their story.

As I entered the refurbished warehouse space where the congregation meets, I noticed hundreds of young adults, many of whom looked to be young professionals, all drinking coffee while waiting to enter the sanctuary. As the worship service started, people began filling up the seats—some in prayerful postures, others lifting their hands in worship. The worship music that day was stirring and powerful, and I was moved by the liturgy of the service, which brought together a beautiful blend of old and new spiritual traditions. From the music, to the sermon, to times of prayer, and the Lord's Table, Trinity Anglican Mission embodied what some call the "three streams" approach to worship, an approach that has come to be known as the Convergence Movement.

At the root of Trinity's three streams expression is their commitment to helping people grow into Christ's image. According to Kris,

> It is our conviction that this approach encourages humility, maturity, and a healthy appreciation for diversity. When we say that we are "evangelical," we mean that we take seriously God's command to speak about and live like Jesus. We preach and teach from the Bible because we believe it is the inspired Word of God, and our desire is for all people to enter into a saving relationship with Jesus. When we say that we are "liturgical," we mean that we value the longevity of historic tradition, the rhythms of the church calendar, the consistency of a lectionary-based teaching plan, and our connection to the global church. When we say that we are "charismatic," we mean that we believe God is present and active among his people. We anticipate the work of the Holy Spirit in the life of the church for the conviction of sin, the illumination of truth, and the restoration of all things.[1]

Since I began investigating churches like Trinity, I have come across dozens of churches that are embracing the three streams approach to ministry and worship. But what is the "three streams" approach? How does it represent a convergence of older and newer traditions?

Three streams churches unite the charismatic, the evangelical, and the liturgical dimensions of the Christian faith into one flowing river of worship. There are churches who come to this from different sides of the aisle. There are traditional mainline or liturgical churches that are embracing charismatic elements into their worship, and there are charismatics who are moving to embrace traditional liturgy. Each side is drawing from the other in an unusual confluence of both old and new. Since one of the distinctive traits of this movement—in contrast to traditional churches and neo-liturgical churches—is a unique focus on the Holy Spirit, let's start by taking a closer look at the charismatic dimension of the three streams movement.

THE SPIRIT AND THE CHURCH

The charismatic work of the Holy Spirit in the church is nothing new. As we scan the pages of church history, we see the Holy Spirit present and working in every era of the church. One conviction uniting the three streams movement is the belief that the Spirit has been in continuous operation since the time of the Old and New Testaments, which is sometimes called a "continuationist" perspective. In contrast, some people today believe that the work of the Holy Spirit ceased with the time of the apostles, but church history seems to tell a different story. The early church fathers such as Justin Martyr (approx. AD 100–165), Irenaeus (approx. AD 120–202), and Tertullian (d. AD 225) all tell of miracles and spiritual gifts of the Holy Spirit and refer to them as a regular practice in the life and ministry of the early church.[2] Bede's *The Ecclesiastical History of the English People*, written in the eighth century, conveys a history of the Christian churches in England and records numerous accounts of miracles and healings.

When we turn to American church history, we learn that the Great Awakening of the eighteenth century was a powerful movement of the Spirit. The Great Awakening began around 1726 as the result of the preaching of theologian Jonathan Edwards and other important Christian leaders. During this time of revival, people experienced an unusual work of the Holy Spirit in their lives, and both young and old were moved to dedicate their lives completely to God. Edwards later wrote an account of the revival, saying, "The Spirit of God began extraordinarily to set in, and wonderfully to work amongst us."[3]

George Whitefield, another leader during the Great Awakening, blazed across North America and the British Isles preaching to countless thousands of people in open fields. Whitefield noted innumerable accounts of people who powerfully encountered the Spirit during these revivals.

John Wesley, a counterpart of George Whitefield and the founder of Wesleyanism, also witnessed a powerful movement of the Spirit both personally and on a national level in Britain and the United States. In 1738, Wesley experienced a personal "heartwarming" conversion at Aldersgate, which marked the beginning of his evangelistic ministry. From that moment, he witnessed an extraordinary outpouring of the Holy Spirit wherever he traveled. Both he and Whitefield believed God was restoring the work of the Spirit in the church through the Great Awakening—and that it was happening right before their very eyes.

The work of the Spirit didn't cease after the great revivals of the eighteenth and nineteenth centuries. In fact, some of the most well-documented and profound movements of the Spirit happened during the charismatic revivals that birthed the modern Pentecostal movement, beginning in Los Angeles, California in the early 1900s. The Azusa Street Revival began when people started gathering to pray for a modern-day outpouring of the Holy Spirit, and as a result, believers were filled with the Spirit, spoke in tongues, and experienced other manifestations. The events at Azusa Street gave rise to the modern Pentecostal movement, and in the nearly one hundred years since that revival, Pentecostalism has become the fastest-growing Christian movement on the planet, crossing denominational and geographic boundaries. Pentecostalism continues to grow at a rate of thirteen million people per year, thirty-five thousand each day, and it has nearly half a billion adherents worldwide. The largest Protestant church in the world is a Pentecostal church in Korea, the Yoido Full Gospel Church, which has over 240,000 people in weekly attendance.

While they are not typically associated with the charismatic church, both the Catholic and Anglican traditions have helped to usher in the charismatic movement in North America and the British Isles. In 1960, Episcopal priest Dennis Bennett announced from the pulpit of St. Mark's Episcopal Church in Van Nuys, California, that he had been filled with the Holy Spirit. This set off a spark that ignited the charismatic renewal in many mainline churches across North America. Around the same time, Michel Harper, a minister at All Souls-Langham Place in London, had a similar experience and became one of the primary leaders of the charismatic movement in the Church of England. The impact of these revivals, and similar ones that followed, continues today.

For example, consider Holy Trinity Brompton (HTB) in London, which is now one of the largest charismatic churches in England. HTB is best known for producing the Alpha Course, which has been used in dozens of countries across hundreds of denominations. The program has helped introduce millions of people to Christ and the ministry of the Holy Spirit. At home, the ministry of Holy Trinity Brompton is reaching several thousand young adults all across London as they replant churches in strategic historic church buildings.

Last year, I attended one of the evening services at HTB. It was an intriguing fusion of the old, the new—and the charismatic. The historic sanctuary was filled with young people; the stage was dark, with smoke machines operating and really loud Christian rock music playing. At the conclusion of the service, I watched as hundreds of young people came to the front for healing prayer. It was ironic, and at the same time refreshing and invigorating, to watch as this congregation brought together modern practices combined with an emphasis on the present-day power of the Spirit in an ancient sanctuary. The church's historic sanctuary offered a sense of God's transcendence, while the contemporary worship and prayer ministry reminded me of the availability of God's power and presence in the world.

Even the Roman Catholic Church has experienced a touch of the charismatic revival. The historic Vatican II Council in the 1960s opened the doors of the church to a new season of innovation, change, and openness to the Holy Spirit, which became known as the Catholic Charismatic Renewal. This movement came to fruition when professors from Duquesne University, a Catholic university in Pittsburgh, attended the Congress of the Cursillo movement in August 1966 and were introduced to *The Cross and the Switchblade* by David Wilkerson, a book that emphasized the work of the Holy Spirit. The next year, several of the professors received the baptism of the Holy Spirit during a prayer meeting, and the movement spread from there to the University of Notre Dame and other places around the country.

Current estimates of the Catholic Charismatic Renewal say that the movement has had an impact in more than two hundred countries, having already touched over 160 million Catholics worldwide, with a large number of those being young adults under the age of thirty. The Charismatic Catholic movement includes an emphasis on a personal relationship with Jesus Christ, baptism in the Holy Spirit, divine healing, and miracles. It is also worth noting that the movement is quite ecumenical, with many of the leaders finding "a natural alliance among these four groups—classical Pentecostals; charismatic denominational Christians; non-denominational charismatics; and Catholic charismatics."[4]

The recovery of the Spirit within the Catholic church has even garnered the recognition of several popes, who have affirmed the contribution of the Catholic Charismatic Renewal. In March 1992, Pope John Paul II affirmed the movement in a statement to the Council of the International Catholic Charismatic Renewal Office:

> At this moment in the Church's history, the Charismatic Renewal can play a significant role in promoting the much-needed defense of Christian life in societies where secularism and materialism have weakened many people's ability to respond to the Spirit and to discern God's loving call.[5]

The current pope, Francis, recently attended the fiftieth anniversary of the Catholic Charismatic Renewal (CCR) in Rome and recognized the significance of this movement and its influence on the larger church:

> Thank you, Catholic Charismatic Renewal, for what you have given the Church in these fifty years! The Church counts on you, on your fidelity to the Spirit, on your willingness to serve and your witness of lives transformed by the Holy Spirit![6]

Today, the charismatic renewal in the Catholic Church has spread throughout the world.[7]

CHARISMATICS EMBRACING LITURGY

We've highlighted the movement of leaders and churches from liturgical traditions in a charismatic direction. But there are also those from within the Pentecostal or charismatic movements who are arriving at a similar place by retaining their charismatic practices while adopting elements of liturgy in worship. In this regard, the work of the late Dr. Robert Webber has been influential. Webber dedicated much of his writing to seeking a balance between charism and liturgy, encouraging many charismatic churches to embrace church tradition. Unlike those who belong to historic traditions such as the Catholic or Anglican church, people in this movement are not bound together by any one jurisdiction. Rather, these churches are a loose federation of congregations that share a common commitment to unifying the three streams.

I recently spent several days hanging out with Glenn Packiam, the pastor of New Life Downtown in Colorado Springs, Colorado. Earlier in his ministry, Glenn was a singer, songwriter, and contemporary worship leader in the nondenominational church movement. More recently, Glenn has been drawn into the stream of historic Christianity, becoming an Anglican priest. I enjoyed learning how New Life Downtown—one of the campuses of New Life Church, a large, multi-site charismatic church in Colorado Springs—has begun structuring their worship around the liturgical patterns of the church.

On his website, Glenn explains why he chose to become an Anglican while still serving in a charismatic church:

> This turn in my journey is not a rejection of the non-denominational church; it is—I hope—a contribution to it. I am called to work within the nondenominational church for a renewal that may come from re-establishing our roots. This is, in fact, a bit of what we are witnessing at New Life. Maybe now I'll be less like a *liturgical thief* and more like that *wise steward* Jesus spoke of who brings out treasures both old and new![8]

Today Glenn is leading the church toward embracing balance, bringing together the "three streams" of the faith: the evangelical, the liturgical, and the charismatic.

Like the neo-liturgical churches we discussed in chapter 4, three streams churches follow the order of Word and table. New Life Downtown describes their worship like this:

We make sense of our identity as the people of God by how we are formed around the Table. We worship at the Lord's Table on Sundays, where we rehearse the gospel and see how blessed we are in Christ. We connect with one another around our tables during the week, where we allow ourselves to be broken, humble, and vulnerable with one another. We serve the church, city, and world by preparing a table for others to meet with Jesus as we become given for the sake of others.[9]

While Glenn's story may sound unusual, it is not an isolated account. Another example of this convergence of the streams is a large charismatic church in St. Joseph, Missouri, called Word of Life Church. Brian and Peri Zahnd founded Word of Life in 1981 when they purchased an old church building with broken stained glass in the hope of reviving the space as a sacred place of worship. Over the years, the church grew exponentially, and in 1996, they constructed a new facility that houses the sanctuary, Solomon's Porch Bookstore & Coffee Shop, the Millennium Youth Center (MYC), and The Upper Room prayer chapel. Yet despite this progress, the church felt something more was still needed, so after a season of fasting and prayer in 2004, Brian led the church through a major transition that included a renewed focus on the cross of Jesus Christ, exploring the mystery of the faith, embracing the history of the church, emphasizing the importance of Christian community, and participating in the revolutionary call to join in God's mission to redeem and restore the world.

Brian's own spiritual journey has influenced much of the church's transition, as he has rediscovered the witness of the historic body of Christ and experienced a growing appreciation for church tradition. Brian shared some pieces of his journey with me:

[It] began with profound discontent that started around the year 2000, not really knowing what to do about it. I began to realize that my experience of Christianity was so pale and thin. I became bored with all the evangelical and charismatic books. It's embarrassing how ignorant I was of the good stuff. I didn't know where to go, so I began to read.

Brian started reading the church fathers in an attempt to back up and start over. Then he began to read philosophy, which grounded him in the nuances of Christian thought. Finally, he began to read from the great works of Western literature, books by Dostoyevsky and others. But it wasn't until he read Dallas Willard's *The Divine Conspiracy* that it all began to come together for him.

In Willard's book, Brian discovered a treasure that enriched his faith and his preaching, and ultimately changed the life of the church. Today he describes himself as a "premodern sacramental eclectic":

> I've learned to worship with my Orthodox, Catholic, Anglican, and mainline brothers and sisters; I've found it beautiful and deeply rewarding. If my circumstances were different, I could imagine myself belonging to any one of these branches of Christianity. As it is, I'm content with being an eclectic Christian . . . or perhaps a premodern sacramental evangelical. What I've found is that within the wide orthodoxy defined by the historic Christian creeds, there is room for a lot of different expressions of our shared faith.[10]

Today, while Word of Life Church is still very much a charismatic church, it has a definite "premodern eclectic" twist to it.

According to Brian, charismatic churches today have reached the end of the road and have exhausted the limits of what can be accomplished by "making it up as you go." Worship leaders are tired of making up their own liturgy, he said, and he believes Pentecostals are well-poised to embrace a more sacramental direction because they have a precedent in practices like the laying on of hands and anointing of the sick. Brian believes leaders just need to be awakened to tradition, and every week he receives calls, emails, and online messages from pastors and Christians who are hungry for more. Brian spoke of a movement happening across the nation where Christians are looking for something with roots, something ancient, and something bigger and deeper. In response to this growing need, he leads a prayer school on developing a personal liturgy, and he has been asked to teach all over the nation and in other countries on this topic.

I asked Brian what convergent worship looks like at Word of Life Church. He described a service of about ninety minutes incorporating a blend of contemporary worship with various elements from church tradition. He said they began to embrace liturgy in small ways and kept adding elements to the worship service over time, like weekly Communion and reciting the Apostles' Creed. Young adults have resonated with this shift at Word of Life. For instance, it was the young people that asked for them to start using ashes on Ash Wednesday. Rather than embracing a full liturgical service, Brian encourages those who want to take a similar path to contextualize liturgy for their own church setting. If you are Pentecostal, he says, then pray for people, and if your tradition has choirs, then use them. The goal is not to replace the DNA of a thriving church, but to add elements of beauty and depth to what's already there. Brian's story is an example of how this can happen as leaders personally search their hearts and study the history of the church.

BRINGING BALANCE TO THE CHURCH

As in previous chapters, we've heard the stories and listened to their hearts of people seeking to recover something they felt was missing from their contemporary church experience. But a question still remains: what can we learn from this movement? Is the future of the church in this embrace of convergence, a blend of the evangelical, charismatic, and liturgical?

Like a gemstone, the Christian life has multiple dimensions or facets. The three streams we've discussed in this chapter represent vastly diverse expressions of the church. Can these streams really work together? Can they offer a deep and meaningful experience of worship? Having walked in the river formed by these three expressions working together, I believe the answer is yes, and I've identified some key takeaways—principles we can apply in any church today.

Balance

Each of the journeys depicted in this chapter is a movement toward the center of Christian expression. We've looked at liturgical streams that have moved in a charismatic direction, and charismatics that have moved toward the liturgical. In both cases, these churches are moving toward one another, and despite their difference in background, they come close to meeting in the middle. They are expressions of *faith seeking balance in praxis*. For charismatics, liturgy and tradition serve as guidelines and guardrails that foster their spiritual experience, while mainline Christians have described the charismatic dimensions they have added to their faith as bringing freshness and vitality. One young person said to me, "I believe that the three streams are especially relevant today because the charismatic, evangelical, and sacramental dimensions of the faith belong together. Each stream is a gift to the body of Christ and belongs to all of us." The convergence of all three addresses different but equally important dimensions of the Christian life, and they are profoundly interrelated, bringing synergy to one another. When the three dimensions are woven together, they offer a balanced model for Christian life and practice.

Many young adults who have been raised in our postmodernism culture naturally seek balance. The modernist tendency toward schism and denominationalism has left many of them with a bad taste, and they are wary of one-dimensional expressions of church that neglect or minimize the contributions of others. Young adults raised in this context often say they felt they were missing a puzzle piece, something that wasn't present in their previous faith expression, but when they embraced the three streams, they found the spiritual balance they were seeking. For many, this convergence has helped bring together the pieces of the spiritual journey into a dynamic expression of the Christian faith.

Unity

The three streams approach has much to offer the church as a pathway toward unity. It can unify Christians as the Spirit works to bring us together (Rom. 15:5–6; Eph. 4:3), and God seems to be using the three streams to bring Christians from various backgrounds and traditions together in worship and mission. In my work for Asbury Theological Seminary, I am privileged to travel widely across the church landscape, and I have a chance to experience the Spirit's work firsthand in different churches and denominations. The charismatic movement has been a spark bringing heat and light to the ecumenical movement, and it has helped bring unity to churches from various backgrounds, especially liturgical and non-liturgical churches.

In a thought-provoking article, theologian Dale Coulter suggests that the three streams can form a bridge into the future for the church:

> The real theological question is whether the sacramental and the charismatic can come together. I think they can because they need each other, and therefore I have hope for the future of global Christianity.[11]

Theologian J. I. Packer implores us to "practice fellowship across the traditions, for the Holy Spirit has been with all God's people in all traditions in all centuries."[12] For many young Christians, uniting the charismatic with the historical is a means of uniting with other believers in a shared spiritual experience of the Holy Spirit.

Spiritual Renewal

As we have seen, the Spirit has been moving in the lives of individuals for centuries. Great men and women of the faith have done extraordinary things when they encounter the power of God's Spirit, and the richness of the Convergence Movement reminds us that we, too, can experience this spiritual renewal for ourselves and in our churches. Is the Holy Spirit still active today? Does he still touch and transform people who diligently seek him? The witness of the three streams movement is a resounding yes!

These churches remind us that the Holy Spirit is real and wants to bring us into a deeper, more intimate relationship with Christ. God has given us the gift of the Holy Spirit to help us live for him and to empower us to be witnesses for Jesus Christ. Jesus promises that we "shall receive power when the Holy Spirit has come upon you; and you shall be witnesses to Me" (Acts 1:8 NKJV). But while Jesus has promised the power, we must *ask* for it! As Dr. David Martin Lloyd-Jones once said, "It is always right to seek the fullness of the Spirit—we are exhorted to do so."[13]

The last few chapters have focused our attention on spiritual journeys within various new, traditional, and charismatic church contexts across North America. In the next chapters will look at how the liturgy offers us practices that can be lived out each day in our personal lives, our homes, and our families. We'll also see how liturgy can be a powerful, formative resource that compels us to reach out to the world in mission.

REFLECTION QUESTIONS AND PRACTICES

- Many people do not associate liturgical traditions with the power of the Holy Spirit. Why is it important that we do not separate the Holy Spirit from these traditions?
- Kris and Glenn are both charismatics who have come to embrace liturgy. What does liturgy hold that seems to have been missing in their previous traditions?
- Did the historic examples in this chapter help you see the charismatic dimension of the faith in a new light? How so?
- What lessons can the church today learn from the three streams approach?

PART 3

PRACTICES

CHAPTER 8

RHYTHMS OF GRACE

*I use the historic practices of Christianity as a
launching pad to propel me into fresh ways and
means, practices, to pursue spiritual transformation.*
TODD HUNTER

We live in a hectic world. Our lives are filled with busy schedules, cell phones, planners, and constant obligations. If we are not careful, our faith becomes just one more thing on our to-do list.

We are also creatures of habit. We have rhythms, routines, and rituals that make up our daily lives (and for many of us, these routines maintain our sanity). We wake up in the morning, drink a cup of coffee, brush our teeth, and read the news. Or maybe we start the day off with a simple prayer and Bible reading. Routines and rituals can be good things!

I want you to think of these routines in your life as liturgies—daily liturgies that keep your life on track and remind you of what matters most. Spiritually speaking, we need to have daily liturgies, rhythms and routines that help us grow in our daily life in Christ. One of the ways we can guard our souls from spiritual burnout is by rediscovering the ancient rhythms of grace that are deeply rooted in the historic Christian faith.

Up to this point, I've focused primarily on unpacking and giving you examples of various traditions. But as we move into the final section of the book, I'd like to make this personal and practical. What are the daily, practical elements of the liturgy—the rhythms of grace that foster spiritual growth and discipleship? In this chapter, we'll transition from looking at corporate liturgical worship to the personal liturgical practices of individual believers. These, too, are important for understanding why young adults are attracted to the liturgy today.

For those of you who are not used to practicing disciplines such as *Lectio Divina* or the daily office, this chapter will offer you a practical introduction to these ideas and practices. You will be able to start your own journey toward learning how to do some of these things. While this is not a complete guide to the spiritual disciplines, I hope to give you enough to whet your appetite for more. I'll hopefully help you see the beauty of these spiritual exercises. And as you learn how to incorporate these practices into your individual worship, they will enhance your corporate worship, too.

Several years ago, I went through a difficult season wherein I felt spiritually exhausted and close to burning out in ministry. Like Bilbo Baggins in *The Fellowship of the Ring*, I felt "thin, sort of *stretched . . .* like butter that has been scraped over too much bread." My evangelical faith had not adequately prepared me for this experience. I grew up attending churches that were skeptical and even suspicious of anything outside of our own beliefs and practices. Thus, I grew up largely ignorant of the classic spiritual practices of the ancient church. While there is much I am grateful for in my evangelical, charismatic heritage, as I reflect back on those days, I see that while my church excelled in helping me know *what* to believe, it did not offer as much help for understanding *how* to practice those beliefs.

Even though I was encouraged to develop a personal prayer life, it was missing a daily liturgy and structure to provide rhythm and routine to the practice. I found myself trying on my own, by myself, and in my own strength to develop a consistent habit. By chance I stumbled across a book on the spiritual disciplines that referenced some of the ancient practices, rhythms, and routines Christians had used in the past. I felt like a stranger entering a foreign land, but as I began to read about the spiritual disciplines, I began to see the beauty of this land. It was a treasure chest from church history, filled with riches waiting to be rediscovered. I discovered prayers that were scriptural and had substance, and although they were old, the words were timeless and full of life. As I began to recover these ancient practices in my personal and private devotions, I sensed a growing, deepening love for God, who is ever ancient and ever new. These ancient practices or rhythms of grace gave me a new sense of balance and stability.

A MAJOR BARRIER: WE'VE SEPARATED BELIEF FROM PRACTICE

We all need spiritual rhythms for our daily lives, whatever those practices may be. Tish Harrison Warren, an Anglican priest in Austin, Texas, speaks to this truth in her recent book *Liturgy of the Ordinary*. Warren peers into the mystery of sacred practices in everyday life and calls us to examine the overlooked moments and routines of our daily lives through the lenses of liturgy. She writes, "The crucible of our formation is in the anonymous monotony of our daily routines."[1] She then argues that the small daily rituals are the ones that form us into who we are, saying, "The often unseen and unsung ways we spend our time are what form us. Our mundane moments, rooted in the communal practices of the church, shape us through habit and repetition . . . into people who spend their days and therefore their lives marked by the love of God."[2]

Habits, whether good or bad, have the power shape our character and mold our will. In his recent book on the power of habits, *You Are What You Love: The Spiritual Power of Habit*, author and professor James K.A. Smith warns that our hearts are being taught to love rival gods through cultural liturgies and daily influences. He gives examples from a visit to the mall, the pervasive nature of advertising, and the rise of social media. These habits are forming us in ways we can't begin to understand. Smith argues that "to be human is to be a liturgical animal, a creature whose loves are shaped by worship."[3] This concept resonates with many young adults who are seeking the recovery of ancient practices, because they recognize that spiritual practices offer a powerful, life-shaping structure that helps counter the constant bombardment of the world's messaging. Young adults I've talked with say they have yearned for the countercultural disciplines of the historic church because those disciplines effectively shape us for another world, for a different way of life. Smith notes that many contemporary churches have failed to reach and keep young adults because the church culture is focused on entertainment rather than spiritual growth. Smith writes, "What passes as youth ministry is often not serious modes of Christian formation but instead pragmatic, last-ditch efforts to keep young people as card-carrying members of our evangelical club."[4] He goes on to discuss the formational value of ancient practices for young adults:

> In my experience, many young people are intensely ritual animals without realizing it. And when they are reintroduced to habit-forming practices of Christian faith, invited into ways of following Jesus that are ancient and tested, their faith is given a second life. They receive the disciplines not as burdensome duties but as gifts that channel their devotion and shape their faith. Instead of relying on their own internal piety and will power (which is a wrong-headed way to think about discipleship anyway), young people experience historic practices of prayer and devotion as gifts of grace in themselves, a way that the Spirit meets them where they are.[5]

Smith hits the target here: young adults (like all of us) are highly liturgical beings who are hungry to be formed through the power of practice. Young adults are looking for daily rhythms and spiritual practices that serve not only as practical outworkings of faith, but also as governing and formational forces in their lives. As one young adult told me, "Culture is currently moving at a mad-dash, frantic pace. Ancient practices root us in the Word and in prayer so that we can ultimately grow to love the things of worship and put aside the things of the world."

We might say that younger Christians are moving away from abstract theory to praxis. When I use the term "praxis" here, I'm referring to spiritual practices of the Christian faith, especially liturgical and spiritual disciplines. This shift has influenced how young people are living out their faith in the local church and in the real world. Jason Brian Santos says, "Ancient and medieval practices have infiltrated the spiritual lives of these generations . . . At the core of this interest, we find young adults longing for something greater than the current offerings on the buffet of the ecclesial marketplace."[6] Theologian, professor, and author Steven Harper writes, "In our day and time we are witnessing a new emergence of the Spirit all over the earth and, along with it, a new commitment to the practice of the means of grace and the keeping of other spiritual disciplines."[7]

The recovery of a disciplined life is in keeping with the apostle Paul's words to his young apprentice: "Discipline yourself for the purpose of godliness" (1 Tim. 4:7 NASB). The word "discipline," which is derived from the Greek word *gumnasia* (from which we get our word "gymnasium"), literally means "exercise," and as we engage in spiritual disciplines, it's like we are essentially exercising our spirituality. That is, just as physical exercise promotes strength in the body, the spiritual disciplines promote godliness and growth in grace. They provide a pathway through which the grace of God transforms us and makes us more and more like Jesus.

Many spiritual disciplines have emerged and been passed like a baton from biblical times through the ages of church history. For the rest of this chapter, we will be examining several ways people are recovering these spiritual disciplines today.

LITURGICAL PRAYERS

We don't always know how to pray. In fact, we don't always feel like praying. In these moments, we need the historic prayers of the church to carry us, providing the words we lack. The young adults I've spoken with often began their liturgical journey by using printed liturgical prayers to help them in their growth and discipleship. I refer to the use of liturgical prayers as a spiritual practice because it is the act of submitting our own spontaneous prayers—often subject to our feelings and wants in the moment—to the written prayers and desires of the church.

There is something beautiful about praying prayers written by others from another time and another place. Doing so provides a connection and continuity with the prayers of other Christians from other times and cultures. These prayers are scriptural and rich in theology, and, although many of them are very old, their words are timeless.

One of the most common ways to begin incorporating written prayers into your devotional life is by using prayer books such as the *Anglican Book of Common Prayer* (sometimes called *The Book of Common Prayer*), a time-tested devotional prayer book that is meant to be used for both the individual and corporate prayers of the church. Its pages are filled with bold, daring, poetic, and rich masterpieces of prayer. A more modern variation of this book is Shane Claiborne and Jonathan Wilson-Hartgrove's *Common Prayer: A Liturgy for Ordinary Radicals*. Claiborne and Wilson-Hartgrove offer a modern prayer book that fuses old and new in an ecumenical expression. In the introduction to the pocket version, Claiborne and Wilson-Hartgrove describe the book as being, "the result of a collaboration of people from many different branches of Christianity, all of which come from one trunk—if you trace the branches all the way back."[8] Prayer books have been my companion on many of my journeys, and they have helped me embrace the rhythms of prayer in my personal life. They offer timeless wisdom for Christians on the road of sanctification.

You may be wondering, why is it called the *Book of* Common *Prayer*? That word, "common," has special significance. Related to our word "community," common doesn't mean "ordinary," rather, it denotes something that is *shared in common with others*. In this sense, the idea of *common* stands in stark contrast to our radically individualistic world, which tends to makes communal prayer not so common. Common prayer draws us into unity as a church, and by praying in the common prayer tradition, we never really pray alone. Whether we are by ourselves in a room, gathered with others in a small group, or are reading the prayers together in a large crowd, our prayers are united with those of other believers both past and present.

Theologian Scot McKnight describes this phenomenon in *Praying with the Church* as he distinguishes between praying *in* the church and *with* the church. Common prayer unites us with other believers around the world who are praying the same rhythms of prayer throughout the day. The body of Christ has always been and will always be a praying church, and common prayer is a way that we can join in the prayers of the saints.

I love hearing the stories of people who have discovered the power of prayer books, but there is one story that stands out from the rest for me. My good friend Morgan grew up in a small Free Methodist Church in upstate New York. Like our friends in chapter 1, Morgan's spiritual journey led him in and out of charismatic churches and, eventually, into the Anglican tradition. Ultimately, it was Morgan's encounter with the *Book of Common Prayer* that was a key factor in leading him to embrace liturgy. He says,

> I came to the prayer book because I was looking for a way to pray. My own words were tired, and I longed for a rhythm of prayer that would connect me with the greater church, both globally and historically. So I bought a prayer book and slowly began to read the words I found on its pages. I stumbled at first, not knowing exactly what to say or what to do. But as I

read the words, and then began to pray the words, those words became my own.

"Those words became my own." This proclamation is a testament to the power of liturgical rhythms. As we engage in disciplined rhythms, we will find that we come to embody the very proclamations we make. This transformative power, the embodiment of our prayers, stands as a testimony of our need for spiritual rhythms.

DISCOVERING THE DAILY OFFICE

At the writing of this book, I have been living in Kentucky and teaching on the campus of Asbury Theological Seminary for three years. During this time, I've noticed something. Every morning and evening, a handful of twentysomethings gather together in the historic Luce Chaperl—a small, intimate chapel on campus—to pray the Daily Office. Morgan helps lead this ministry of morning and evening prayer. He said, "Through the morning and evening offices, the prayers of the church wove their way into my being and transformed the way I relate with the world. These prayers have formed a personal liturgy that frames my time, morning and evening, and continues to point me to the sacredness of God's work in a simple, ordinary day."

For centuries, Christian believers have employed this wonderful tool known as the Daily Office to help structure their prayers. The Daily Office—sometimes called the "Divine Office"—is based on the ancient practice of prescribing or scheduling daily times of prayer. The name is derived from the Latin *officium divinum*, meaning "divine office" or "divine duty." It originates from the Jewish practice of daily prayer as outlined in the Old Testament. As time passed, the Jewish people began to follow Torah readings, psalms, and hymns at fixed hours of the day, and drawing from this routine, early Christians began to order their prayer life around specific times of the day.

By the second and third centuries, early church fathers such as Clement of Alexandria, Tertullian, and Origen had written about the practice of the Daily Office and its implementation among gatherings of believers. In monasteries, these prayers were implemented in both individual and group settings. Over time, the discipline of praying at scheduled times or hours has spread throughout the church and around the world.

As Morgan has, many young adults have found that praying the Daily Office helps add a sense of regularity and balance to their prayer life. They use it privately in dorms and bedrooms and corporately in coffee houses and classrooms. You can use the Daily Office at your own pace. It's a wonderful way to center yourself in the morning before you begin your busy day, and it can help calm you as you prepare for the hours of the night. As you follow the Daily Office, you'll want to take it slowly, getting into the rhythm of praying both morning and evening. Like millions of other Christians through the centuries, you may find praying through the Daily Office to be a unique and enriching personal experience. If you'd like to see an example of what the daily office looks like, you can view a sample of morning and evening prayer in the appendix at the back of this book.

PRAYER OF THE EXAMEN

When it comes to baking, my wife Kay is our family expert. I'm the first to admit that I can't bake for anything, so when I came across the book *Out of the House of Bread* by Preston Yancey in our local bookstore, I immediately bought it for my wife. Preston is a millennial, raised as a Southern Baptist, who recently became an Anglican. The book turned out to be a treasure, not only for her, but for me as well. Preston invites readers to walk with Jesus through the practices of spiritual disciplines by connecting the disciplines with the everyday task of baking bread. One chapter in particular, on the ancient practice of reflective prayer called the *examen*, stood out to me. Preston helped me better understand how this simple prayer, designed to help us cultivate the practice of examining ourselves at the end of each day by noting the highs, lows, and emotions we have experienced can be vital for spiritual growth. As with many of the disciplines, it may feel unusual at first, but with practice it can be a healthy recipe for spiritual growth and vitality. He writes, "The practice of the Ignatian Examen is just that—practice."[9]

The practice of the prayer of examen goes back more than five hundred years to St. Ignatius of Loyola, who encouraged a practice of prayerful reflection on the events of the day in order to detect God's presence and to discern his direction. Although it is Roman Catholic in origin, many people—both young and old—are using this simple reflective prayer. The examen can be practiced in a group or by yourself, and it is suggested that you find fifteen minutes during your daily routine to review the last twenty-four hours using this practice. Below is a sample version of the examen from Jim Manney's book *A Simple Life-Changing Prayer.*

1. Pray for Light.
2. Begin by asking God for the grace to pray, to see, and to understand.
3. Give thanks.
4. Look at your day in a spirit of gratitude. Everything is a gift from God.
5. Review the day.
6. Guided by the Holy Spirit, look back on your day. Pay attention to your experience. Look for God in it.
7. Look at what's wrong.
8. Face up to failures and shortcomings. Ask forgiveness for your faults. Ask God to show you ways to improve.
9. Resolve what to do in the day to come.
10. Where do you need God today? What can you do today?[10]

Lectio Divina

Another ancient practice that many young adults are rediscovering is *Lectio Divina*. *Lectio Divina* is a meditative way to read a passage of Scripture and pray at the same time. It reminds us that prayer and Bible study are inseparably linked, and that Scripture should always be read in the context of prayer. Prayer is the medium that brings us into contact with the same Holy Spirit who inspired the authors of the Bible. As we read the Scriptures, the Spirit applies the truths of the Word to our hearts. Prayer is the necessary means whereby we understand the Word of God, because without the assistance of the Holy Spirit in prayer, our Bible study will be in vain.

Lectio Divina is a form of meditation. Because prayer and studying the sacred Scriptures are important for growing in our faith, we practice immersing ourselves daily in the sacred texts. In Hebrew thought, meditating on Scripture means quietly repeating it, giving oneself entirely to God, and abandoning outside distractions. This understanding lies behind the meaning of the Hebrew word we commonly translate as "meditate" in Psalm 1:2. We are told to meditate on two things: the Word of God and the goodness of God. Paul affirms this when he writes to the Philippians, "Whatever is true, whatever is noble, whatever is just, whatever is pure, whatever is lovely, whatever things are of good report . . . *meditate* on these things." (Phil. 4:8 NKJV). *Lectio Divina* is a practical, time-tested method of reading the Bible, and it has held a special place in the church through the centuries. It is a means of connecting with God through a personal experience of meditation on his Word.

In a world filled with distractions, we need a quiet place where God can speak to us. Many people spend only a few minutes each day reading and meditating on the Bible, and often this isn't enough. Sitting and prayerfully meditating on God's Word put the cares of this world in proper perspective and opens us up to allowing God to speak to us. Unlike some forms of meditation, *Lectio Divina* doesn't advocate emptying the mind. Instead, we practice freeing our minds from distraction so that we can fill them with God's Word.

What does this look like in practice? Simply choose a short passage of Scripture and meditate on it, allowing it to sink into your heart and soul. We see a biblical picture of the art of *Lectio Divina* in the story of Mary and Martha in Luke 10:38–42. In this story, Mary sits at the feet of Jesus and listens to him, while Martha is distracted with the cares of serving. Jesus says that Mary chose the better way because she prioritized him and did not consume herself with the distractions of the world. *Lectio Divina* follows the example of Mary by encouraging us to sit at the feet of Jesus and hear his Word. *Lectio Divina* reminds us that words matter to God, and therefore they should matter to us. God has ordained his Word to be a means of communion with him, and *Lectio Divina* helps us to clearly hear and respond to the God who spoke the world into existence.

SILENCE AND SOLITUDE

Another ancient practice growing in popularity today is the discipline of silence and solitude. These are related practices that should be engaged together; one without the other is incomplete. Recently I spoke with Mike King, president of Youthfront, a youth ministry that hosts retreats for over four thousand youth each year. He shared that during his decade of work with young people, he has found that the combination of "silence and solitude is the queen of the practices." He said, "Silence and the quiet are essential for young people to recover. We need to give them space to listen to themselves and the Holy Spirit." Mike said many young people are beginning to include silence as a part of their daily routine of prayer, starting with a few minutes each day. Others find quiet time by taking a day-long, silent retreat once a week or monthly. Elizabeth, a twentysomething, told me silence is essential for her spiritual growth and formation. She practices a period of silence every day. "At first trying to practice silence was difficult since I had grown accustomed to noise always being around me," she said. "However, I have cultivated silence as an essential part of my daily time with God. It has been life changing!"

We live in a world of noise, and with the abundance of messages we constantly encounter today, words have in many ways lost their meaning. We encounter messages in print, on signs, on billboards, on the TV, on our computers and phones. We scan Facebook, and Twitter and quickly read our emails and text messages. The average American is bombarded with over three thousand advertising messages every day. One danger of living in this flood of messages is that they drown out the unique Word we need to hear from God. More than ever, we must learn to cultivate times of silence, and there is no better way to develop this discipline than by pairing it with time alone in solitude.

One result of practicing silence is the empowerment of our own words. When we pause to experience silence, we begin to value and appreciate the spoken word. Sadly, our prayers tend to be shallow, selfish, and lacking any serious reflection on the nature of God. We need prayers that arise from a deep place in our hearts, an experience of God shaped by silence and solitude. These practices help us pray more thoughtfully, staying focused on God and his kingdom.

Do you remember the old Simon and Garfunkel song, "The Sound of Silence"? All too often, we hear without truly *listening*. Times of silence enable us to listen to the still, small voice of God. We find this practice modeled by Jesus, who would often depart from the crowds to spend periods in silence and solitude, alone with the Father. Consider the following Scriptures:

- "He went up on the mountain by Himself to pray. Now when evening came, He was alone there." (Matt. 14:23 NKJV)
- "He departed and went into a deserted place." (Luke 4:42 NKJV)
- "So He Himself often withdrew into the wilderness and prayed." (Luke 5:16 NKJV)

- "He went out to the mountain to pray, and continued all night in prayer." (Luke 6:12 NKJV)
- "He went up on the mountain to pray." (Luke 9:28 NKJV)
- "He went out and departed to a solitary place, and there He prayed." (Mark 1:35 NKJV)
- "He departed to the mountain to pray." (Mark 6:46 NKJV)

It might be cliché to say this, but it is still true: if Jesus was a proponent of this practice, perhaps it is something we should consider for our own lives today.

RECOVERING ANCIENT PRACTICES TODAY

The practices I've mentioned in this chapter represent several of the essential ancient practices young adults are recovering to help them grow deeper in their relationship with Jesus. There are, of course, other such practices we could explore like the spiritual pilgrimage, the rule of life, the use of icons, centering prayer, and journaling. For a more detailed examination of these and other spiritual practices, I recommend Richard Foster's classic book *Celebration of Discipline.*

Some Christians may be concerned that these ancient practices are too structured, that they might not allow for the freedom of the Spirit, but I would argue that the opposite is true. Like a vine growing on a trellis, they provide us with a structure for our faith to grow, not a straitjacket that binds us. Spiritual practices lay a foundation that keeps us grounded while freeing us to be open to the leading of the Holy Spirit. These ancient practices anchor the soul and provide tangible ways for people to build their faith and to grow in Christ.

Now, these ancient practices are certainly not the only way Christians should practice their faith. They are not requirements for being a faithful Christian. However, these practices are habits and disciplines that have enriched the faith of millions of Christians around the world for hundreds of years, and they can help us develop a vibrant, healthy, life-giving faith today. Becoming a mature disciple of Christ doesn't just happen. The Christian faith is more than a theory taught in a classroom; it's something we practice and embody in everyday life. Spiritual disciplines are not for a select group of dedicated people, but for all Christians: pastors, professors, or plumbers! Let's commit ourselves to the process of discipleship by practicing spiritual disciplines in our everyday lives.

REFLECTION QUESTIONS
AND PRACTICES

- Why is a rhythmic life important?
- So many of us have grown up in church traditions that have separated belief from practice. How can the recovery of practices help us live out a holistic, embodied faith?
- How does liturgy give us practices that shape our faith and formation?
- If you haven't done so already, look to create a rule of life for yourself that helps you foster your own rhythms. For good examples, see Peter Scazzero's *Emotionally Healthy Spirituality* and Ruth Haley Barton's *Sacred Rhythms*.

CHAPTER 9

CONNECTING LITURGY AND MISSION

The church has missionary power in direct
proportion to its liturgical integrity.
STANLEY HAUERWAS

Many contemporary Christians see liturgy as an outdated impediment to the church's mission. The archaic language and ancient rhythms are associated with static, stale spirituality. The stereotype is a church stuck in the past, focused on itself, and largely irrelevant to today's problems.

While this may apply to some churches in the liturgical tradition, I want to challenge this stereotype. What if liturgy could serve as a launching pad rather than a detriment to our mission? In my study of the neo-liturgical and neo-monastic movements and the renewed interest in liturgy among young adults, I've become convinced that there is a forgotten way here, one that the church of today needs to recover. For this recovery to be successful and fruitful, it requires connecting the liturgical and missional elements together.

When understood properly, I believe the DNA of the liturgical tradition can prepare and compel believers to join in the mission of God. As the church begins to realize the holistic connections between discipleship and evangelism—seeing them as two sides of the same coin—we can begin to see how liturgy has a missional element that forms Christians to embrace mission, to look outward. From Saint Francis and his monks in Italy, to Ignatius of Loyola and the Spanish Jesuits, to Augustine and the mission to England, there are many examples of this "liturgical mission" in the history of the church.

But these are examples from different times and places. What about today? Can something from the past be relevant in our scientific, technological world? The answer is a resounding "Yes!" Thousands of Christian churches are rediscovering the essential connection between liturgy and mission, and throughout this chapter I will share some concrete examples of how this generation is reaching the world through mission rooted in liturgy. My hope is that this chapter will surprise you, dismantle some of your stereotypes, and inspire you to join Jesus in his mission to the world. Strap on your seat belts, and let's see how the Lord is raising up a new generation of believers for liturgical mission.

LITURGY AS A LAUNCHING PAD

To begin, I want to explore how a service constructed according to the historic fourfold order (Gathering, Hearing, Feeding, Sending) of liturgical worship fosters a posture of mission. One of the best-kept secrets of liturgy is found in the final words of the service: "Go! You are sent!" Although they come at the end of the service, these words don't mark the end of our sacramental journey, but instead mark the beginning of our missional activity in the world. The liturgy of the Word and table have prepared us for this.

The order of the service calls us out of the world and forms us through the proclamation of the word and the receiving of God's grace in Communion. This formation, in turn, leads to the people of

God being sent back into the world. The words spoken at the end—"Go! You are sent!"—remind us that the purpose of our gathering is *to answer the call of God to reenter the world with the Word of God on our lips.* We are reminded through the words of the liturgy that we are called to bear witness to the living Christ in the power of the Holy Spirit and to see our lives as an extension of Christ's ongoing mission in the world. These are more than nice words; they remind us what it means to be the church.

Still, the concluding words are often one of the most overlooked aspects of the church's life and liturgy, leading some to wonder, "Do liturgy and mission go together?" Western culture tends to divide the spiritual from the physical. Orthodox theologian Alexander Schmemann, in his book *For the Life of the World*, writes, "The Western Christian is used to thinking of sacrament as opposed to the Word, and he links the mission with the Word and not the sacrament."[1] Schmemann tries to offer a more intergrated view of the church wherein liturgy, mission, and sacrament are not viewed as separate and distinct from one another but as interconnected and related. Taken together, they are at the heart of what the church is and does:

> The Church is the sacrament of the Kingdom—not because she possesses divinely instituted acts called "sacraments," but because first of all she is the possibility given to man to see in and through this world the "world to come," to see and to "live" it in Christ. It is only when in the darkness of this world we discern that Christ has already "filled all things with Himself" that these things, whatever they may be, are revealed and given to us full of meaning and beauty. A Christian is the one who, wherever he looks, finds Christ and rejoices in Him. And his joy transforms all his human plans and programs, decisions and actions, making all his mission the sacrament of the world's return to Him who is the life of the world.[2]

The church is the embodiment of Christ's mission in the world. It is formed by the message of the kingdom and tasked with embodying kingdom ideals—both inside and outside the walls of the church.

We may struggle to makes these connections. What does it mean to bring the "sacrament" into the world? Again, Schmemann encourages us to recover the liturgical and sacramental life of the church. Rather than seeing mission as something the church does *apart* from its liturgy, we must see that mission begins in liturgical worship, "for it alone makes possible the liturgy of mission."[3] His phrase, "the liturgy of mission," is a reminder that liturgy, when rightly understood, should always lead to the sending activity of the church. The liturgy of a sacramental service is designed to prepare us for how we live in the world, and it ends with the command to go into the world. The liturgy is intended to form us for the Great Commission each week.

Bishop Todd Hunter presses in further on the design of the liturgy when he asks, "Using liturgy as a launching pad, how can we engage in the spiritual practice of liturgy in a way that leads to the work of the people outside the four walls of a church building, in public space?"[4] Ever since Creation, God has given a mission—a task for which they bear responsibility—to his people, and today the church stands as the people of God sent into the world to join God's work of redemption and restoration. To unpack what that looks like in the real world, let's consider some examples of liturgical mission we find today.

LITURGY AND SOCIAL JUSTICE

Many young people today are enamored by what is commonly called "social justice," a reference to actions taken on behalf of those who are oppressed or marginalized by society. A large percentage of young adults are joining or starting social enterprises and nonprofits that serve the physical needs of marginalized people.[5] Yet a divide persists in many evangelical Protestant circles between those committed to "evangelistic mission" and "social justice."

I've spoken with many young adults who do not see the divide as sharply as prior generations. They are eager to integrate the two ideals and find that this integration is easier in some of the liturgical traditions. This should not be surprising, because there is a historic connection here between liturgy and our mission in the world. Today we may call it "social justice," but it is really just another extension of God's mission to reclaim everything in his kingdom.

Many Christians in the evangelical tradition have tended to view mission in narrow terms: the saving of souls, sometimes at the expense of physical or material needs. But a liturgical faith encourages a holistic approach, marrying the physical, emotional, and spiritual into one. Rejecting the bifurcation of heart from mind and body, younger generations are seeking ways to unite these, and liturgy offers us help. The sacramental nature of liturgy naturally ties the spiritual to the physical, reminding us that God's work is not limited to one or the other, but consists of both working together.

This unity, a reintegration of mind, body, and soul, cannot help but lead to a renewed awareness of the need for social justice. Again, a sacramental understanding of the faith fosters this integration. The Word of the Lord commissions us not only to save souls, but to care for those around us who cannot care for themselves or do not have a voice of their own. Jesus said, "Truly I tell you, whatever you did for one of the least of these brothers and sisters of mine, you did for me" (Matt. 25:40). Many young adults today are heeding the call of Jesus to care for the "least of these" in society. As one young adult said to me, "Before finding the liturgical tradition, going to church had always been about me and my needs. Since I began attending my small liturgical church, I have come to realize that worship isn't about me, but about God. Taking the Lord's Supper each week has opened me up to the needs of the world as well in a very beautiful way." When our worship focuses on the beauty and magnificent nature of God, we can't help but shift our eyes outward and see the world through the love and compassion of God. We see people made in the image of God to care for instead of souls to count in order to increase our numbers.

THE SACRAMENT OF COFFEE: RWANDA

In 1994, the East African nation of Rwanda experienced one of worst genocides in history. Over the course of just one hundred days, close to one million ethnic Tutsis and moderate Hutus died at the hands of extremist Hutus. The Rwandan genocide left millions of innocent people orphaned or widowed, many of them young children and elderly. In the face of such evil, it's hard to imagine something good coming to light, but there were glimmers of hope in the aftermath as the government called upon the church to help bring healing and reconciliation between the Tutsi and Hutu and to work together to eradicate poverty and illiteracy. Seeing the aftermath and devastation, one company, led by an entrepreneurial leader in the US, offered hope to those in Rwanda.

In 2005, Jonathan Golden developed a simple way to bring together people from around the world and help rebuild the Rwandan economy. Golden started a coffee company that would pay fair wages to Rwandan farmers and bring a quality product to coffee lovers. The results have been nothing short of amazing. Since 2005, Land of a Thousand Hills Coffee has become a multi-million-dollar company. It provides better than fair wages to more than 2,500 Rwandan farmers and their families, helping them rebuild their nation and work together toward lasting peace. Before he began this work, Golden asked a Rwandan bishop how he could best help the people of Rwanda. The bishop said, "Show them you love them by what you do first—then talk about Jesus second."

Jonathan shared with me that his work is about showing, not telling. It is an opportunity to live out the gospel in an incarnational way, one that *shows* the love of Christ in addition to telling people about it. It might surprise you to learn that Jonathan is also an Anglican priest and a church planter. His liturgical faith has influenced his international coffee company in a powerful way. In contrast to the simple conversionist model of church, Jonathan begins with the idea, "If you can break bread with us, you can be a part of us. Come and pray with us. Liturgical mission is less words and more action." This view of mission has influenced everything he does, and it is imbedded in the DNA of his company.

Jonathan sees his work as an extension of liturgy, one that unites people together. When we get up in the morning and make a cup of coffee, it is a ritual. It is a liturgy that transforms the beans into the coffee we drink, the final step in a process. Yet this is only the final piece of a larger process—from farmers planting the bushes and taking care of them so that they reap beans, to the picking and processing of those beans, to their shipment, roasting, brewing, and drinking—that links us all together in a cycle of mutual dependence and support for one another. Something as routine as a cup of coffee becomes a sacrament because it unites us with farmers around the world. Our coffee consumption supports them so they can earn a fair living. Jonathan's slogan for the company is simple, and he has invited millions to "Drink Coffee. Do Good."

THE OPEN DOOR: MONTRÉAL, CANADA

Over the last two years, I have made several trips to Montréal to meet with young adults engaged in significant mission work there. After breakfast one morning, my friend Mark Dunwoody asked if he could show me something. Nothing could have prepared me for our walk to an old Anglican church building. To my surprise, the building was filled with homeless men and women, some sleeping in pews, others drinking coffee to ward off their hangovers from the night before. I was amazed and overwhelmed at how this ancient church building was hosting a mission for society's forgotten.

The Open Door provides services to homeless and low-income people in downtown Montréal, from providing food, clothing, and shelter during the day to referrals for professional mental health and drug addiction counselors, and employment assistance. In many ways, The Open Door is providing the light and love of Christ to their patrons. According to their website, "Our initial goal is to see that the primary needs of clients are met. From there we begin building them up and empowering them."[6]

As we walked around the church, Mark introduced me to one of the leaders, Zack Ingles. Zack is twenty-seven years old and has a warm smile. He has also had an interesting faith journey, one that has included leading worship in charismatic churches, working in over ten different church denominations, and finding a home in the Anglican Church of Canada. What struck me was his genuine love for people who are typically viewed as outcasts by society. When Zack and his wife moved to downtown Montréal, he began looking for a job. A friend gave him The Open Door's number. Zack's subsequent phone call was life-changing. He was moved to tears as he entered the hundred-year-old church building for the first time. It was filled with homeless people sleeping on the pews and covered in wool blankets and eating at tables.

Zack sees The Open Door's work as an embodiment of the connection between liturgy and mission. He shared that the prayers, words of the liturgy, and the Lord's Table all remind us of our own need for the living bread of Christ: "Give us this day our daily bread," "Feed my sheep," "When you do it unto the least of these you do it unto me." There are many phrases and metaphors in Scripture that remind us of God's love for the poor *and* of our own spiritual need for God. Zack sees how these needs—*both* spiritual and physical—are more intertwined than we think.

Zack believes liturgy and its sacramental worldview reminds us of our calling us to be risk-takers, to get out of our comfortable boxes and to care for the oppressed and hurting. Working at The Open Door has given Zack a new way to express his understanding of the church's mission. He said, "I would like the church to take the gospel seriously and begin to take risks, rather than staying safe." Zack lives this "risky" mission every day as he faithfully serves the poor of Montréal. His life is a reminder that God calls us to provide the Bread of Life *and* the bread people need to live. For Zack, mission is about heaven meeting earth, a reality most clearly celebrated in the sacraments. The liturgy he experiences on Sunday prepares him for his mission in the world—working at the intersection of heaven and earth the other six days of the week.

PLANTING NEW LITURGICAL CHURCHES

For the last decade, I have been involved in planting missional churches across North America. I currently serve as the director of church planting at Asbury Seminary, where I help train church leaders who belong to a variety of denominations and networks around the world. Some of the most exciting and innovative forms of mission are among those who embrace the liturgical traditions. In recent years, I've witnessed a wave of new churches of all shapes and sizes with one thing in common: they are recovering liturgical practices for the express purpose of spiritual formation in a postmodern and post-Christian context.

One example is Village Church in Greenville, South Carolina. We met its founder, Seth Cain, in an earlier chapter. After graduating from Wheaton College, Seth moved back to the South, where he and his wife eventually planted Village Church on the distressed west side of Greenville. Seth describes Village Church as "a creative and compassionate Anglican community, worshiping God, and serving our neighbors on the Westside,"[7] with a vision to connect the areas of worship, community, and mission in a unified whole. Seth and Village Church have recently moved into a beautiful, historic Methodist church building in downtown Greenville. The church has become a powerful witness to the community and an example of how a new church can be both liturgical and missional.

I've also had the pleasure of meeting church planter Shawn McCain, who calls himself a "sacramental church planter." While he was studying at Fuller Theological Seminary, Shawn and his wife stumbled into a liturgical church and began to discern a call to plant a liturgical and sacramental church in Santa Cruz, California. Shawn said, "After a year of planning and praying, it became clear there was a much bigger movement of God underway. Since then, we've teamed up with other families to plant two more churches in Asheville, North Carolina and Austin, Texas."[8] They are now a few years into planting Resurrection South Austin Church in Austin, Texas, and have come to realize they are not alone, that there is a movement of sacramental mission happening all over the country. McCain said their Resurrection "draws together the rich ancient/future heritage of the Christian faith that enables us to embody, proclaim, and demonstrate the gospel in ways that change us and benefit others."[9]

Seth's and Shawn's stories are not isolated. Across the country dozens of new churches are embracing liturgy and mission. Though it may not be scientific, a simple Google search using the words "liturgical sacramental church planting" turns up over four hundred thousand results. There is a fresh movement of new churches that are both liturgical and missional, and that number is growing daily.

A FEW TAKEAWAYS

What can we learn from these stories and examples? Is there an inherent link between liturgy and mission? Here are a few final takeaways for you.

Liturgy Forms Us for Mission

For many of the young adults I've interviewed, liturgy provides a foundation for living a life focused on mission. In other words, there is something in the very structure and spirit of liturgy that prepares us to be people on mission in the world. Week after week, day after day, the prayers and words of the liturgy and the tangible elements of the sacraments nourish and prepare us for mission. We can have confidence knowing that God created us for the spiritual rhythms found in these practices.

Disillusionment with Modern Worship Services

Some young adults I spoke with said they were disillusioned with contemporary worship services because of the focus on entertainment. They were turned off by sermon titles urging them to "live your best life now" and worship services that resemble rock concerts. One young adult said, "I am tired of being entertained. I want to be *fed*. I have found that liturgy feeds me in ways that a good sermon by itself never could. Liturgy provides a balance of Word and table that forms me each week." Another young adult poignantly shared a frustration with the individualism of the typical church service: "The liturgy isn't about me, but about God and his world. Each week I am being formed for mission through the liturgy." Again and again, I heard young people alluding to the connection between the sacrament of the Lord's Supper and how it prepares us to go back out into the world on mission.

Find Your Own Calcutta

One last suggestion: *Find your own Calcutta.* If you want to get involved, find a place where you can minister to those who desperately need the gospel. Mother Teresa inspired the world by her radical commitment to serve the poorest of the poor in Calcutta. Thousands of people came from around the world to offer their help to her, yet she told many of them, "Find your own Calcutta." In other words, be who God created you to be, wherever you are, whether that means being a good brother or sister, parent, or neighbor. Every story of mission is different because each person is unique, and the liturgy of mission is about becoming who you are before God. Thomas Merton once said, "For me, to be a saint means to be myself."[10] Every one of us can play a part in God's sacramental mission because we have been sent as missionaries to share the gospel in our own culture and context.

The liturgy of mission reminds us that church is not an end in itself. The church is sent into the world to fulfill the mission of God. This is a great challenge, and each of us must ask ourselves: "Where is my Calcutta? Where can I serve, right now, in the place I already live?" Seek to bring God's kingdom justice to that place as you bridge the gap between the physical and spiritual needs of the people around you. In doing this, you aren't alone! You are joining the thousands, perhaps millions, of people today who have taken the sacramental ethos present in the liturgy and carried it out into the world on mission.

In saying this, however, we must never forget that the liturgy is not ultimately about us. It is rooted in the life, death, and resurrection of Christ. It is *this* reality that compels us to be the church in the world on mission. This historic truth can offer a holistic framework for everyday Christian living, discipleship, and mission in the twenty-first century. In this chapter I've offered a brief introduction to the ways we can bridge the gap between liturgy and mission in the hope that it will stir your thinking and provoke further action. May the church of today draw inspiration and wisdom from the past to reach out in the ever-changing context of postmodern culture.

REFLECTION QUESTIONS
AND PRACTICES

- I mentioned above that many people assume that liturgical churches don't engage in mission. Have you heard this stereotype before? If so, what are some examples you have encountered?
- How does liturgy compel us to participate in God's mission for the world?
- Did either Zack or Jonathan's stories inspire you to reconnect mission with liturgy? How?
- I found Mother Teresa's exhortation to "Find your own Calcutta" to be very powerful. How do you see this advice coming to life in your own faith?

CHAPTER 10

BRINGING LITURGY HOME

*The domestic church has its own liturgy that
echoes and points to the universal church.*
MSGR. RENZO BONETTI

I first met Henry and his family at our local Anglican Church. Henry is originally from California, and he has served on staff at several large Pentecostal churches. When he and his family originally moved to the Lexington area to teach and pursue a doctoral program at the University of Kentucky, they began to look for a new church home. They wanted to try something different. As Henry said to me, they had been burned out on "super-spiritual and superficial Christianity." After visiting a number of churches around town, a neighbor invited them to attend our Anglican church, and they were intrigued to see what it would be like. Not knowing what to expect, they loaded up their minivan and came to the service together, as a family. To their surprise, rather than finding a stuffy, boring church service that the children hated, they found an oasis of worship where their entire family met God through the liturgy. The words, prayers, and celebration of the Eucharist allowed each member of their family to engage in the worship, and week after week they returned for more. After a few months, they knew there was no going back, and they joined the church.

As I've visited churches across the country, I've been continually amazed at how many young families are embracing liturgy together. Many of these churches are intergenerational, and the vast majority of families I've encountered come to these liturgical churches from non-traditional backgrounds. Liturgy is new to them, but they've found something unique and attractive in it. Why are they involving their families in the liturgical tradition? You might be surprised to hear that one of the main reasons is to encourage family-based discipleship and formation.

When my own family moved to Kentucky a few years ago, we visited all kinds of churches in order to find the "right one." This experience was somewhat traumatic for our family, leaving us exhausted and on the verge of giving up. We finally decided to visit a nearby Anglican church (the same one Henry and his family attend now). Our children sat through the entire service, and when the time came to go forward to receive Communion, we all went together and knelt at the Communion rail to receive the body and bood of Christ. I remember thinking: *Could this be it? Could this really be the church for us?*

After the service, as we piled into our van and asked our girls what they thought, our then eleven-year-old Anna Belle summed it up by saying, "It doesn't get any better than that!" We've been going back ever since. After months of searching, our family finally felt like we had found a home, one where we all could participate in the worship together.

WHY ARE YOUNG FAMILIES EMBRACING LITURGY?

For most of this book, we've looked at the allure of liturgy for young adults, but we haven't addressed how liturgy connects with young families. As you might guess, I've heard many positive examples of families who are embracing liturgy together. Based on my own observations as a husband and a father of three girls, and on my conversations with other young families, I want to suggest a few reasons why liturgy matters to families. My hope is that this short chapter will encourage you to bring at least one liturgical element into your life together as a family. If you are a single person reading this, or don't have young children, many of the insights in this chapter can also apply to discipleship in small group settings of various sizes.

Liturgy Invites Participation

As we've noted several times, much of contemporary Christianity is focused on entertainment, and this seems especially true with regard to children's ministries. A family goes to church for an hour and a half, sits and listen to music, then listens to a sermon. Many times the family is segregated by age, with the children attending their own service. Most of the time, all you need to do is show up and watch. Church worship is something done for you, and this tends to create a passive, consumerist Christianity where the church is "all about me" and my wants and my needs. The church can easily become yet another vendor of goods and services, instead of being a place where we are challenged to grow, serve, give, and go back into the world in mission. Sadly, although we bring our children to church hoping they will be formed by the counter-cultural values of God's kingdom, in many of our services, our children are being raised from an early age to embrace consumerism.

In addition, the segregation of families as they enter the building encourages individualism, yet many families want to resist this and practice their faith together. One of the most common reasons parents feel drawn to liturgy is that it involves the whole family worshiping together. The focus of the liturgical service is not on the parents or the children, but on God, the church, and the world. In most liturgical churches, families are encouraged to worship together during the singing portion of the service, and then many churches dismiss children but make sure they return to rejoin their parents prior to the Lord's Supper so that the family can partake of Communion together.

In one such church, a young father said to me, "I love that we can worship together as a family. Before finding our liturgical church, we never felt like our children were wanted in the service. But now, it is the norm." Another young parent told me that what she liked best about the liturgy was that their family gets to worship together: "This is a new and wonderful experience for all of us," she said.

This approach also resonates with children. After we started going to the Anglican church we now regularly attend, I asked my three young daughters Elizabeth, Anna Belle, and Caroline—ages fourteen, eleven, and five—what they thought about the liturgy. In their own words they shared that they like the familiarity of knowing what's coming next because it enables them to fully participate in the service. My girls shared that visiting churches can be scary if you don't know what is going to happen during the worship service. With the written liturgy, they can easily follow along. They enjoy feeling like they belong because they are able to pray the same prayers as the rest of the congregation.

Several of the parents I spoke with emphasized the power of participation in the Eucharist together as a family. In many evangelical churches, Communion feels like an add-on to the service, something unusual that only happens a few times a year. In most liturgical churches, Holy Communion is celebrated every week, and families see the Lord's Supper as a powerful reminder of the corporate unity of being a part of the body of Christ both locally and universally rather than as a dead ritual. One parent said to me, "As we come to the Lord's Table, we are reminded that our family is a part of a larger family of believers. Each week we share the same table with millions of Christians around the world." My wife, Kay, agrees. She says the Holy Spirit meets us as a family during the Communion time.

The Repetition of Words

Learning theory tells us that one of the best ways to learn is by repetition, saying words and phrases over and over, and that children learn best by establishing these kinds of routines. Liturgy forms our faith through prayers that are repeated again and again. The repetitive nature of liturgy allows the words and prayers to sink deep into the hearts and minds of children. Week after week, day after day, the words become a part of the very fabric of their lives.

My wife, Kay, has repeatedly said she appreciates the repetitive nature of the liturgy: "The repetition of the liturgy is a beautiful thing that builds in us and our children a foundation of the faith. It trickles into their souls as they say those words each week in the liturgy and throughout the week as we pray together as a family." She highlights the Apostles' Creed and the Lord's Prayer as two key examples of formative repetition that we recite week after week during worship and in our times of daily prayer as well. The Apostles' Creed gives us words of faith to affirm together as a family. Kay has said she notices how the words sink into children's memories and how their minds are expanded because of them. One day they will be able to affirm their faith because of saying those words over and over throughout their childhood years.

Kristi Durban is another young mother whose family has recently embraced liturgy. She and her husband, Trevor, have found that liturgy helps bind and form them together as a family, and they have seen their children benefit from the routine. The rhythms of the church calendar and the seasons help to ground spiritual practices through annual repetition as well. In Kristi's words,

> What is attractive about liturgy as a family is that the liturgy can help our kids discover the faith as full of meaning and beauty. The liturgy acts as a teacher to us all. Subsequently, I recognize that training my children up in the way of the faith does not rest wholly on my (imperfect) abilities, but that the liturgical life of the church is also a teacher and guide to my children.

The Lord's Prayer is a powerful prayer for families to learn together. It is the most important and historically significant prayer of the Bible and one of the most popular passages of Scripture, often read at funerals, weddings, and church services throughout the Christian world. According to Kay, "It can help shape both our personal and family prayer life. In our home, we pray the Lord's Prayer together at dinner and before bed every evening. Many times, our girls will lead us in saying the Lord's Prayer." The church we attend says the Lord's Prayer on Sunday mornings during worship, and our children are also encouraged to pray it together during Sunday school.

Practices for Home Life

Liturgy isn't just for Sunday morning, of course, but what does this look like in practice? Young families are finding that the liturgical tradition provides them with simple, practical ways to help them bring their faith home. Similar to how we gather for liturgical worship in church on Sundays, we can also come together in the home for times of family worship that involve liturgical practices of prayer, reading Scripture, and singing songs together. The practices a family selects may vary, and some adapt ancient practices in different ways to ground their busy lives and schedules. One family who recently became Eastern Orthodox, for example, has an icon corner in their house where they gather together every night to light a candle and pray the ancient prayer called the *Phos Hilaron*, which means in English "O Gladsome Light." I've included it here so you can get a feel for what this type of practice is like—at least on paper:

> O Gladsome Light of the Holy Glory of the Immortal Father, Heavenly, Holy, Blessed Jesus Christ! Now that we have come to the setting of the sun and behold the light of evening, we praise God, Father, Son and Holy Spirit. For meet it is at all times to worship Thee with voices of praise. O Son of God and Giver of Life, therefore all the world doth glorify Thee.

Other families have found that the weekly lectionary readings offer a refreshing routine of Scripture for everyday life. Don't underestimate the power of the daily reading of Scripture! It not only helps ground your family in a shared experience of the Word, but daily readings provide encouragement for the week. Many families are intimidated because they don't know what verses to read or even how to read the Bible, but the lectionary takes care of that. It provides you with verses, offering a harmony between weekly worship and Bible reading in the home. The weekly lectionary readings become our family verses, and we use them to meditate upon throughout the week in our devotional times together. There are a number of online lectionary resources, including the Revised Common Lectionary page by Vanderbilt Divinity School.[1]

Some families are also experimenting by creating their own liturgies for morning and evening prayer. One young father told me, "My wife and I have adapted our own family prayers from the *Book of Common Prayer*. We simplified the prayers so that our children can say and understand them as well." In our home we pray a prayer from the compline service of the *Book of Common Prayer* that reads, "Guide us waking, O Lord, and guard us sleeping; that awake we may watch with Christ, and asleep we may rest in peace." Regardless of what prayers you use, family liturgy can be a wonderful way to bring faith into your home.

Dr. Jonathan Powers, professor of worship at Asbury Seminary and father of two young daughters, believes in the power of the liturgy to form families in the home. He says, "When done correctly, liturgy serves as a catechesis whereby people's lives are transformed through their growth in knowledge, behavior, virtue, prayer, and practice as well as delight in God. The goal of liturgical catechesis is the formation of healthy Christians who will go out and grow the kingdom in healthy ways. Such holistic formation through liturgy requires a multitude of practices both inside and outside the church, many of which must start in the home." The liturgical tradition offers parents and families a wealth of practices that help bring discipleship and formation from the church into the home.

Recovering Sabbath Rest

We all want more time, but we never seem to have enough of it. Another reason families are embracing liturgy is that it helps them recover time. Liturgy follows the Christian calendar, which calls us out of our secular time orientation and orders the annual cycle of our lives around the life of Christ. These rhythms and distinctions conform us to Christ within a worshiping context, and they help us regain the Sabbath as a day of rest. Setting apart Sunday as a holy day of worship can free us from our addictions to technology and media, because liturgy encourages us to value reflection and contemplation. I once heard a mother say, "Liturgy gives room for quiet and silence in worship, which we so desperately need in this stage of life."

Recovering the Sabbath is a key rhythm for many families. Many shared how discovering liturgy reinforced the importance of taking a day for the Lord—and for their family together. This is necessary today because families are busy with school, sports, and endless activities, and they rarely have extended time together. Sabbath rest allows time each week for spiritual rest and solitude from busyness and distractions. Our souls need rest the same way our physical bodies need rest, and if we are not careful, we will experience spiritual burnout. God promises rest to his people, and this conveys the idea of a resting place, a quiet place, one where we find peace, trust, and reliance upon God. Rest is why God commanded us to keep the Sabbath, and we need our rest if we are to continue to be a part of his mission.

Structuring Life around Seasons

I am writing this chapter during the season of Advent, my favorite season of the liturgical Christian year. I love everything about Advent, especially the colors and smells. Advent reminds me of the mystery of the virgin birth of our Savior Jesus Christ. The season of

Advent also marks the beginning of the church year for Christians all over the world. During Advent, we prepare our hearts for the mystery of the incarnation by focusing on the virgin birth and the faith of the Virgin Mary, the shepherds, and the wise men.

One of the things I love most about Advent is how it brings us together as a family. We have begun developing our own family traditions, and during Advent we light the candles of the Advent wreath and read Scripture and prayers together each week. We love attending church together to refocus and be reminded of the true meaning of the season. All the seasons of the Christian year have been a wonderful discipleship tool that we have used to celebrate the major events of the life of Jesus.

Kristi Durban, who I introduced earlier, said several aspects of the church calendar have been helpful for her family as well. She notes that during holiday seasons we can easily succumb to the pitfalls of commercialism, emotionalism, or spouting empty platitudes. But the seasons of the church lead us to focus on more than just one day, and we can enjoy an entire season to prepare ourselves—our hearts, our minds—for that day. During Advent we look forward to Christ's birth, but we take time to truly *wait* with anticipation. When Christmas arrives, we don't get as wrapped up (pun intended) in the gifts, but instead celebrate Christ, the one we have been waiting for during the preceding weeks. Each marker and season offers a touch point for the family, an invitation to conversation and shared spiritual life with prayer or reading or other commemorative actions. Kristi went on to say,

> The seasons invite us to slow down and place our hearts' and minds' focus on God. For our family, church traditions have inspired us to implement practices in our home that center around the seasons of the church year. These traditions have allowed our spiritual lives to be fully integrated between Sunday worship and every other day of the week. Faith is not relegated to one day of the week and forgotten; the traditions

we practice in church and which spill over at home help our kids to see God as a part of everyday life, every moment.

The seasons of the church year can also be a helpful way for families to celebrate the major themes of the gospel of Jesus Christ in their homes with their children.

TEACHING OBEDIENCE AT HOME

All of life is liturgical. Whether you realize it or not, you perform hundreds of rituals every day that have sacramental significance. Our homes, our families, and our daily rituals all have liturgical meaning. Your home is a "domestic church," a term the early church used to describe the natural connection between the church and the family unit. Catholic Msgr. Renzo Bonetti says, "The domestic church has its own liturgy that echoes and points to the universal church."[2] The rituals and practices of the home are liturgies that should flow from the rituals and practices of the church. The liturgy of the family means that the home is also a place of Christian worship, learning, and discipleship. We bring the components of a worship service—which includes reading the Bible, praying, and singing—into our homes through family liturgy.

Thinking about our homes as domestic churches is a radical paradigm shift for many of us in the West. Too often, we think of the church as a babysitting service to watch our kids for a few hours a week. But nothing could be further from the truth! And while church is important, the Bible tells us that the home is the primary place of learning the Bible and giving moral instruction. In Deuteronomy 6:5–9, Moses outlines the responsibilities of parents, activities that clearly have sacramental significance and meaning:

> You shall love the LORD your God with all your heart, with all your soul, and with all your strength. And these words which

I command you today shall be in your heart. You shall teach
them diligently to your children, and shall talk of them when
you sit in your house, when you walk by the way, when you lie
down, and when you rise up. You shall bind them as a sign on
your hand, and they shall be as frontlets between your eyes.
You shall write them on the doorposts of your house and on
your gates. (NKJV)

This passage is a paradigm for what Bonetti calls "the liturgy of
the family," a liturgy that begins *with us* and *in us*. The "words which
I command you today shall be in your heart" is a message for parents.
This is not just something we do for the kids, but something we
participate in alongside of them. In the liturgy of the family, parents
and children alike are shaped into disciples of Jesus Christ through
shared words, prayers, rituals, and routines.

The liturgy of the family reminds us that faith is not just something we do once a week, but something we should incorporate into
the daily routines of the home. There is perhaps no better place to
do this than the dinner table. Through the sharing of meals with
one another, our homes become sacred places of hospitality and
thanksgiving that echo the sacrament of the eucharistic celebration.
Something as simple as a bowl of soup or a grilled cheese sandwich can become sacramental if it is made and received with love.
Commenting on the act of making sandwiches for his children,
Andre Dubus observes,

A sacrament is physical, and within it is God's love; as a sandwich is physical, and nutritious and pleasurable, and within
it is love, if someone makes it for you and gives it to you with
love; even harried or tired or impatient love, but with love's
direction and concern, love's again and again wavering and
distorted focus on goodness; then God's love too is in the
sandwich.[3]

Finally, the liturgy of the family is not meant to be confined to the home, but to be lived out in our communities. As we saw in the previous chapter, mission flows from liturgy, and in the same way, the liturgy of the family begins in our homes, but it also compels us to touch our neighbors with the love of Christ. One of the most powerful witnesses we can offer the world is to live out our faith together as a family. Most non-Christians have no idea what it means to be a Christian family, and they will not know the difference unless they see it in our families. Jesus said, "By this all will know that you are my disciples, if you have love for one another" (John 13:35 NKJV). The liturgy of the family and the love we share is a powerful witness to the world, and the world desperately needs to know and see what a Christ-centered family looks like.

REFLECTION QUESTIONS AND PRACTICES

- Why do you think liturgy is relevant for family-based discipleship?
- Why is it important for entire families to practice their faith together?
- How does the liturgy provide a foundation for practices for ordinary daily life?
- What is one practice mentioned in this chapter that you could begin to implement in your own life whether you are single or married?

EPILOGUE

*The geographic pilgrimage is the symbolic
acting out of an inner journey.*
THOMAS MERTON

We have reached the end of our time together. Throughout this book, I've tried to introduce you to a few of the young adults and church leaders I've met over the past several years. We've tried to understand why they are drawn to liturgy and its ancient practices. I began this book by reflecting on my own journey. After reflecting on my own journey, I wanted to hear the journeys of others, and my search has both deepened my own understanding and appreciation of liturgy and ancient practices, as well as my love for the young people I've met. It has confirmed for me that I am not alone in seeing the ongoing relevance and blessings of liturgy for the twenty-first century.

That said, I don't want to give the impression that this translates into a hope that we can reverse the decline of traditional mainline churches in North America, Canada, and England. A wide variety of church leaders I've spoken with—bishops, archbishops, and even a cardinal of the Catholic Church—have all agreed that what we are seeing is not a mass movement of young people flocking to the church, but a resurgence among youth who are seeking greater faithfulness to Christ and his church. While it is true that a small number of young adults are becoming Catholic, Eastern Orthodox, and Anglican, the vast majority of those I interviewed are remaining in their non-traditional churches and adapting and incorporating the practices of liturgy into their existing context. They are embracing a fresh expression of the faith, one that is a creative synthesis of old and new for the twenty-first century.

Chris Backert is the national director of Fresh Expression US, and he agrees that this renewed interest in liturgy does not mean a wholesale embrace of the traditional, historic churches of Christianity. Most of these young adults are staying in their Protestant, evangelical churches and are borrowing from church tradition rather than fully embracing it. The takeaway from this is that you don't have to join a liturgical tradition to have access to liturgy. Many are finding that sacramental practices can be appropriated in the free-church tradition as well. In his work with denominations across the United States, Chris sees how churches in non-liturgical traditions are drawing wisdom from church tradition and incorporating that into their own context.

Perhaps the real hope for the church is not in going backward, but in a convergence of old and new that paves a way forward. The late Robert Webber, one of the forerunners of today's ancient-future faith movement, once wrote, "The road to the future runs through the past." For many of these young adults, embracing liturgy isn't about reliving the past, it's about retrieving it and appropriating it into the context of life in twenty-first-century North America. As Martin Smith states, "Faithfulness to tradition does not mean mere perpetuation or copying of ways from the past but a creative recovery of the past as a source of inspiration and guidance in our faithfulness to God's future."[1] A liturgical faith is not about reverting back to "the good ol' days," but is a way for the past, present, and future to come together for a new generation.

While the past provides us with an abundance of wisdom concerning how to make disciples, we must also be actively engaged with our modern context. Contextual theology is theology that is formed in a unique context, and younger generations are embracing a contextual liturgy that takes into consideration the local social climate. The stories of these young adults remind us that the future of the church not only lies in the traditions of the past, but in the unique implementation of these concepts in our world today. In the words of Leonard Sweet, "Postmodern Pilgrims must strive to keep the past and the present in perpetual conversation so every generation will find a fresh expression of the Gospel that is anchored solidly to the faith that was once delivered."[2] I believe the future of the church will be found on the road where the past and the present meet.

MORE THAN MERE THEOLOGY AND EXPERIENCE

In the previous pages we've seen a variety of individuals whose spiritual journeys have taken them in, out of, and back to the church. They are on a path looking for something bigger, larger, older, richer, and fuller than themselves and their own generation. They are searching for the transcendent and have refused to quit searching, despite finding many of modern expressions of worship to be lacking a full expression of faith.

Many of those who have experienced the power of liturgy and the ancient practices have done so by trying other expressions of Christianity before finding a home in the historic liturgy. This is the reason why I have often referred to this as a "journey," because so many young adults have dabbled in different traditions and have found unique beauty within each of them. Ultimately, many walk away feeling that no specific expression of the faith is truly complete. Some have tried Pentecostal/charismatic traditions for the experience, but this wasn't enough. Others have tried liberal, progressive Christianity, attracted by its inclusivity, but this wasn't enough. Still others have turned to the liturgical traditions and have found them wanting in various ways. Perhaps the real lesson for us here is that no single tradition is able to capture the fullness of what it means to be the church today. Taken alone, none of them are sufficient for the deep, holistic formation so many young people are seeking.

A LITURGICAL MATRIX

While theology alone, experience alone, and tradition alone will not form you, when these are combined, we have biblical discipleship. When we embrace liturgy *in conjunction with* good theology and experience of God in community, it reinforces what we believe and forms us for obedience to God. We need a liturgical matrix that brings together orthodoxy (right doctrine), orthopraxy (right practice), and orthopathy (right experience) in a way that leads to lasting transformation, and I believe the ancient liturgies and practices of the church are foundational for ensuring that our practices are forming us to be mature disciples of Jesus. Liturgy is for living; it is the "work of the people." What we believe influences our worship, and how we worship influences what we believe. Good liturgy forms us to live our daily lives with the overflow of the love of Christ, and liturgical practices bring together the best of all these gifts into a synergy of faith and practice for daily living.

Liturgy gives us a foundation to build our life practices upon, one that is rooted in a renewal of God's redemptive story. What we need most of all today is a resurgence of liturgical tradition that is alive and gives us practices to help us express and live out our faith. On a personal level, liturgy and ancient practices help us live out Christian faith on a daily basis—week in and week out—as they help us create sacred rhythms. They provide daily practices for prayer and spiritual growth, and weekly rhythms of liturgical worship that are connected to an annual cycle whereby we can follow Jesus through the church calendar. We can be fed in a more tangible way as we come to the table, cleansed as we remember our baptism, and healed as we receive prayer from our community of faith. As Brian Zahnd says, "We need the whole body of Christ to properly form the body of Christ. This much I'm sure of: Orthodox mystery, Catholic beauty, Anglican liturgy, Protestant audacity, Evangelical energy, Charismatic reality—I need it all!"[3]

I believe the most powerful benefit of recovering the liturgical tradition for this generation is that it offers a holistic framework for understanding how life beyond Sunday morning service is sacramental. Liturgy, when rightly appropriated, is one of the best ways for us to make disciples in a postmodern context. Liturgy infuses our doctrine, our worship, our practices, and our community with sacramental significance, reminding us that the kingdom of God is where we live. It's the meeting of heaven and earth. Recovering this is at the heart of recovering a historic Christian faith. The allure of liturgy isn't just a passing fad or the latest gimmick; it represents a longing for roots that connect us to another reality, a world set apart that runs parallel to our modern age. It's a longing for ancient practices that form our faith and connects us to the larger body of Christ, preparing us for God's mission in the world. The recovery of liturgical practices among this generation is a sign of revival, a Spirit-inspired movement that should give us hope for the future of the church as it rediscovers its ancient roots.

A prayer of Saint Augustine is still fitting for us today. It is a prayer that embodies the spirit of Christ followers in every generation as they long for God—the one who *is ever ancient, ever new.*

Late have I loved you, O Beauty ever ancient, ever new, late have I loved you! You were within me, but I was outside, and it was there that I searched for you. In my unloveliness I plunged into the lovely things which you created. You were with me, but I was not with you. Created things kept me from you; yet if they had not been in you they would have not been at all. You called, you shouted, and you broke through my deafness. You flashed, you shone, and you dispelled my blindness. You breathed your fragrance on me; I drew in breath and now I pant for you. I have tasted you, now I hunger and thirst for more. You touched me, and I burned for your peace."

ACKNOWLEDGMENTS

Very few books are written in isolation by one person alone, rather they are often a liturgical "work of the people" involving the influence of others. *Ever Ancient, Ever New* is no exception. I would like to acknowledge several key people who have influenced me in writing this book on the recovery of liturgy among this generation.

First, I would like to thank my wife, Kay, and our three daughters, Elizabeth, Anna Belle, and Caroline, for taking this liturgical journey with me. I am so thankful that we get to do life and faith together. I love you all so much!

I would like to thank the dozens of young adults who allowed me to interview them for the book. They inspired my writing this book, and I believe they represent the hope for the future of the church. I am especially thankful for several of my former Asbury Seminary students, Ross Jenkins, Morgan Clark, and Lindsey Runyan, who helped encourage me in the early phases of this project. I am so proud of each of you!

I would like to thank the entire Zondervan publishing team. It has been a great joy and honor working with everyone on the book from start to finish. I would especially like to thank my editor, Ryan Pazdur, who first reached out to me and believed in the project. This book wouldn't have been possible without him. I would also like to thank Chad Harrington for his editorial assistance on the manuscript and Harmony Harkema for helping get the book ready for publication.

I would like to thank author and theologian Scot McKnight for the thoughtful foreword and for all the many ways he has helped this generation through his teaching and his writing. Thank you so much!

Finally, I'd like to thank the eclectic group of saints past and present who have helped me see the importance and vitality of liturgy for today. Writers like C. S. Lewis, N. T. Wright, J. I. Packer, Robert Webber, James K.A. Smith, and Todd Hunter have helped ground me in the richness of this tradition. I would like to also acknowledge friends and leaders Steve Wood, Kris McDaniel, Charles Gill, Cheryl Bridges Johns, Martin Gornick, and many others who have been a light along the way.

NOTES

Foreword

1. Alan Jacobs, *The Book of Common Prayer: A Biography* (Princeton: Princeton University Press, 2013), 194.

Introduction

1. For an in-depth study on the spirituality of youth and young adults see Christian Smith and Melinda Lundquist Denton, *Soul Searching: The Religious Lives and Spiritual Lives of American Teenagers.* (Oxford: Oxford University Press, 2005), and Christian Smith and Patricia Snell, *Souls in Transition: The Religious and Spiritual Lives of Emerging Adults* (Oxford: Oxford University Press, 2009). Their findings show that the majority of youth adhere to a vague understanding of religion they call Moralistic Therapeutic Deism (MTD). For statistics on the overall state of youth involvement in religion in North America, the Pew Research Center has observed that about a third of older millennials (adults currently in their late twenties and early thirties) now say they have no religion, up nine percentage points among this age range since 2007. Nearly a quarter of Generation X now say they have no particular religion or describe themselves as atheists or agnostics. See http://www.pewforum.org/2015/05/12/americas-changing-religious-landscape/.

2. Todd Hunter, *Accidental Anglican: The Surprising Appeal of the Liturgical Church.* (Downers Grove, IL: InterVarsity Press, 2010), vii.

3. Robert E. Webber, *The Younger Evangelicals: Facing the Challenges of the New World* (Grand Rapids, MI.: Baker Books, 2002), 179.

4. Steven Croft, Ian Mosby, and Stephanie Spellers, *Ancient Faith, Future Mission: Fresh Expressions in the Sacramental Tradition* (New York: Seabury Books), 108.

Chapter 1: The New Search for Liturgy

1. This chapter does not allow enough room to fully discuss the shift from modernity to postmodernity. For a more detailed discussion, see Robert E. Webber, *Ancient-Future Faith: Rethinking Evangelicalism for a Postmodern World* (Grand Rapids, MI: Baker Academic, 2003), 13–25. For a Christian perspective on the impact of postmodernism on the church and culture, see James K.A. Smith, *Who's Afraid of Postmodernism?: Taking Derrida, Lyotard, and Foucault to Church* (Grand Rapids: Baker Academic, 2006). Smith argues that the philosophies of French thinkers Derrida, Lyotard, and Foucault, which form the basis for postmodern thought, actually have a deep affinity with Christianity. See also other books in the Church and Postmodern Culture series at www.churchandpomo.org.

2. Jason Brian Santos, *A Community Called Taizé: A Story of Prayer, Worship and Reconciliation* (Downers Grove, IL: InterVarsity Press, 2008), 149.

3. Leonard Sweet, *Soul Tsunami: Sink or Swim in the New Millennium Culture* (Grand Rapids, MI: Zondervan, 1999), 17.

4. "America's Changing Religious Landscape," Pew Research Center, May 12, 2015, http://www.pewforum.org/2015/05/12/americas-changing-religious-landscape/.

5. Diana Butler Bass, *Christianity after Religion: The End of Church and the Birth of a New Spiritual Awakening* (New York: Harper Collins, 2013), 46.

6. Rachel Held Evans, *Searching for Sunday: Loving, Leaving, and Finding the Church* (Nashville: Thomas Nelson, 2015), xiv.

7. James K.A. Smith, personal interview and email, November 16, 2017.

8. Tom Beaudoin, *Virtual Faith: The Irreverent Quest of Generation X* (San Francisco: Jossey-Bass, 1998), 164.

9. See Thomas G. Long, *Beyond the Worship Wars: Building Vital and Faithful Worship* (Bethesda, MD: The Alban Institute, 2001).

10. Robert Webber, *Evangelicals on the Canterbury Trail: Why Evangelicals Are Attracted to Liturgical Church* (Grand Rapids, MI: Baker Books, 1985), 47.

11. Rachel Held Evans, *Searching for Sunday*, (Nashville: Thomas Nelson, 2015), xvi.

12. Patricia Hendricks, *Hungry Souls, Holy Companions* (Harrisburg, PA: Morehouse, 2006), 6.

13. Todd Hunter, *Giving Church Another Chance: Finding New Meaning in Spiritual Practices* (Downers Grove, IL: InterVarsity Press, 2010), 32.

Chapter 2: The Power of Liturgy

1. M. Robert Mulholland, *Invitation to a Journey: A Roadmap for Spiritual Formation* (Downers Grove, IL: InterVarsity Press, 1993), 177.

2. Mark Galli, *Beyond Smells and Bells: The Wonder and Power of Christian Liturgy* (Brewster, MA: Paraclete Press, 2008), 13.

3. Massey Shepherd, Jr., *Liturgy and Education* (New York: Seabury Press, 1963), 98.

4. Patrick Malloy, "Rick Warren Meets Gregory Dix: The Liturgical Movement Comes Knocking at the Megachurch Door," *Anglican Theological Review* 92.3 (Summer 2010), 449.

5. John Stott, *Between Two Worlds: The Art of Preaching in the Twentieth Century* (Grand Rapids, MI: Eerdmans, 1982), 15.

6. Many of the early Church Fathers spoke about the regularity of the Eucharist in the church's life and worship, including Cyprian, Ambrose, Basil, and Chrysostom, who wrote about the Eucharist as a daily practice in the life of the church.

7. Compare Acts 2:42–46 with Paul's use of the word *koinonia* in 1 Corinthians 11:20–34.

8. Luke Timothy Johnson includes this observation in his discussion on Jesus in the memory of the church. He says, "*Anamnesis* in earliest Christianity was even more complex, for the one remembered from the past was also being experienced as present

here and now", *The Writings of the New Testament* (Minneapolis, MN: Fortress Press, 1999), 125.

9. Marcus Borg and N. T. Wright, *The Meaning of Jesus: Two Visions* (San Francisco, CA: Harper Collins, 1999), 207.

Chapter 3: Surprised by Orthodoxy

1. Christian Smith and Melinda Lundquist Denton, *Soul Searching: The Religious and Spiritual Lives of American Teenagers* (New York: Oxford University Press, 2005), 118–171.

2. Cited in Rod Dreher's *The Benedict Option* (New York: Sentinel, 2017), 10.

3. Gracy Olmstead, "Why Millennials Long for Liturgy: Is the High Church the Christianity of the Future?" *The American Conservative*, Jan. 14, 2014, http://www.theamericanconservative. com/articles/why-millennials-long-for-liturgy.

4. Colleen Carroll Campbell, *The New Faithful: Why Young Adults Are Embracing Christian Orthodoxy*, (Chicago: Loyola Press, 2002), 15.

5. Ibid., 15–16.

6. Ben Irwin, https://benirwin.me/2015/01/22/11-things-about-the -episcopal-church/.

7. A quick search of the internet reveals this link between technology and depression in young adults. See David Volpi, "Heavy Technology Use Linked to Fatigue, Stress and Depression in Young Adults," Huffington Post Blog, August 2, 2012, http://www.huffingtonpost .com/david-volpi-md-pc-facs/technology-depression_b_1723625 .html. Also see Alison Jones, "More Technology Use Linked to Mental Health Issues in At-risk Adolescents", Duke Today, May 3, 2017, https://today.duke.edu/2017/05/more-technology-use-linked -mental-health-issues-risk-adolescents.

8. Ben Irwin, https://benirwin.me/2015/01/22/11-things-about-the -episcopal-church/.

9. C. S. Lewis, *Mere Christianity* (New York: Collier Books, 1952), vi.

10. G. K. Chesterton, *Orthodoxy* (New York: Barnes & Noble, 2007), 5.

11. Michael Ramsey, *The Anglican Spirit* (New York, NY: Seabury Classics, 2004), 7.

12. See http://newcitycatechism.com/.
13. J. I. Packer and Gary A. Parrett, "The Lost Art of Catechesis: It's a Tried and True Way of Teaching, Among Other Things, Christian Doctrine," *Christianity Today*, March 12, 2010, http://www.christianitytoday.com/ct/2010/march/14.26.html.
14. Ibid.
15. See Howard Snyder, *The Radical Wesley: The Patterns and Practices of a Movement Maker* (Franklin, TN: Seedbed, 2014).
16. Alister McGrath, "The Tradition Continues," *Christian History Magazine*, Issue 48, 40.
17. John Stott, *The Living Church: Convictions of a Lifelong Pastor* (Downers Grove, IL: InterVarsity Press, 2007), 161.

Chapter 4: The Appeal of the Ancient Traditions

1. Bede, *A History of the English Church and People* (London: Penguin Books, 1968), 44.
2. Elizabeth Peterson, "Can I Watch You Pray?" *Anglican Journeys*, Anglican Pastor, March 5, 2015, http://anglicanpastor.com/anglican-journeys-elizabeth-peterson/.
3. Matthew Schmitz, "The Kids Are Old Rite," Catholic Herald, August 31, 2017, http://catholicherald.co.uk/issues/september-1st-2017/the-kids-are-old-rite/.
4. "Unchurched Prefer Cathedrals to Contemporary Church Designs," LifeWay Research, April 4, 2008, https://lifewayresearch.com/2008/04/04/unchurched-prefer-cathedrals-to-contemporary-church-designs/.
5. Joel Connelly, "Compline: An Ancient Service Draws the Young," Seattle Politics, Nov. 19, 2013, http://blog.seattlepi.com/seattlepolitics/2013/11/19/compline-an-ancient-service-draws-the-young/.
6. The icon that so captured my imagination during mother's time in the hospital was *The Icon of Christ* by Theophanes of Crete (1546).

Chapter 5: The Quest for Community

1. William H. Shannon and Christine M. Bochen, eds., *Thomas Merton: A Life in Letters* (New York: HarperCollins, 2008), 350–51.

2. See Joan Chittister, *The Rule of Benedict: A Spirituality for the 21st Century*, 2nd ed. (New York: Crossroad, 2010).

3. "Community," Taizé, https://www.taize.fr/en_rubrique8.html.

4. Patriarch Bartholomew, "Speech During the Common Prayer," Taizé, https://www.taize.fr/en_article21840.html.

5. Ibid.

6. See http://stanselm.org.uk/.

7. Rachael Lopez, "A Tangible Connection: Finding New and Ancient Ways to Pray," St. Anselm Online, Jan. 18, 2017, http://stanselm.org.uk/a-tangible-connection-finding-new-and-ancient-ways-to-pray/.

8. "Who We Are," The Simple Way, http://www.thesimpleway.org/about.

9. Ibid.

10. Jonathan Wilson-Hartgrove, *New Monasticism: What It Has to Say to Today's Church* (Grand Rapids, MI: Brazos Press, 2008), 39.

11. Martin Luther, *Table Talk* (New York: Dover, 2005), 35.

12. Aelred of Rievaulx, *Spiritual Friendship* (Collegeville, MN: Cistercian Publications, 2010), 38.

13. Wesley Hill, *Spiritual Friendship: Finding Love in the Church as a Celibate Gay Christian* (Grand Rapids, MI: Brazos Press, 2015), xx.

14. Rod Dreher, *The Benedict Option: A Strategy for Christians in a Post-Christian Nation* (New York: Sentinel, 2017).

Chapter 6: Something Ancient, Something New

1. "What to Expect," Imago Dei, http://idcraleigh.com.

2. John Starke, "TGC Asks: How Do You Use Liturgical Elements in Your Church Worship?" The Gospel Coalition, April 24, 2011, https://www.thegospelcoalition.org/article/tgc-asks-how-do-you-use-liturgical-elements-in-your-church-worship.

3. "Our Story," Pangea Church, http://pangea.church/our-story/.

4. Ibid.

5. Matt. 26:26–27; Mark 14:22–23; Luke 22:17–19; 1 Cor. 11:20–24.

Chapter 7: Three Streams, One River

1. For more information, see the Trinity Anglican website at https:// atltrinity.org.

2. For a more in-depth introduction to the spiritual gifts in the early church, see Ronald A. N. Kydd, *Charismatic Gifts in the Early Church: The Gifts of the Spirit in the First 300 Years* (Peabody, MA: Hendrickson Publishers, 2014) and Chris Armstrong, "Signs and Wonders: The Charismatic Power of Early Christianity," Christianity Today online, Jan. 2009, http://www .christianitytoday.com/history/2009/january/signs-and-wonders -charismatic-power-of-early-christianity.html.

3. Jonathan Edwards, *Jonathan Edwards on Revival* (Carlisle, PA: The Banner of Truth, 1984), 12..

4. "Statement on Year of Jubilee 2017," Catholic Charismatic Renewal National Service Committee, http://www.nsc-charis center.org/statement-on-year-of-jubilee-2017/.

5. "Address of His Holiness John Paul II to the Council of the International Catholic Charismatic Renewal Office," March 14, 1992, https://w2.vatican.va/content/john-paul-ii/en/speeches/ 1992/march/documents/hf_jp-ii_spe_19920314_charismatic -renewal.html.

6. "Vigil of Pentecost and ecumenical prayer with Pope Francis at the Circus Maximus on the occasion of the Golden Jubilee of Catholic Charismatic Renewal," Holy See Press Office Bulletin, June 2017, https://press.vatican.va/content/salastampa/en/ bollettino/pubblico/2017/06/03/170603g.html.

7. For more information on the Catholic Charismatic Renewal, see http://www.nsc-chariscenter.org/.

8. Glenn Packiam, "Why I'm Becoming an Anglican Priest . . . at New Life Church," personal blog, Mar. 2, 2014, http://glenn packiam.typepad.com/my_weblog/2014/03/why-im-becoming-an -anglican-priest.html.

9. "Christ Centered and Gospel-Shaped," New Life Downtown, http://www.newlifechurch.org/downtown.

10. Brian Zahnd, "A Premodern Sacramental Eclectic," personal blog,

June 24, 2013, https://brianzahnd.com/2013/06/a-premodern-sacramental-eclectic/.

11. Dale Coulter, "A Charismatic Invasion of Anglicanism?" *First Things*, Jan. 7, 2014, http://www.firstthings.com/blogs/first thoughts/2014/01/neither-an-invasion-nor-surprising-lambeth -palace-chemin-neuf-and-anglican-charismatics.

12. J. I. Packer cited in Roger Steer, *Guarding the Holy Fire: The Evangelicalism of John R.W. Stott, J. I. Packer, and Alister McGrath* (Grand Rapids, MI: Baker Books, 1999), 218.

13. David Martyn Lloyd-Jones, *The Sovereign Spirit* (Wheaton, IL: Harold Shaw Publishers, 1985), 48.

Chapter 8: Rhythms of Grace

1. Tish Harrison Warren, *Liturgy of the Ordinary: Sacred Practices in Everyday Life* (Downers Grove, IL: InterVarsity Press, 2010), 34.

2. Ibid., 32.

3. James K.A. Smith, *You Are What You Love: The Spiritual Power of Habit* (Grand Rapids, MI: Brazos Press, 2016), 23.

4. Ibid., 145.

5. Ibid., 147.

6. Jason Brian Santos, *A Community Called Taizé* (Downers Grove, IL: InterVarsity Press, 2008), 151.

7. Steven Harper, *A Pocket Guide to Prayer* (Nashville: Upper Room, 2010), 7.

8. Shane Claiborne and Jonathan Wilson-Hartgrove, *Common Prayer Pocket Edition* (Grand Rapids, MI: Zondervan, 2012), 13.

9. Preston Yancey, *Out of the House of Bread* (Grand Rapids, MI: Zondervan, 2016), 44.

10. Jim Manney, *A Simple, Life-Changing Prayer: Discovering the Power of St. Ignatius Loyola's Examen* (Chicago: Loyola Press, 2011), 81–82.

Chapter 9: Connecting Liturgy and Mission

1. Alexander Schmemann, *For the Life of the World* (New York: St. Vladimir's Seminary Press, 1963), 21.

2. Ibid, 113.

3. Ibid, 46.

4. Todd Hunter, *Giving Church Another Chance* (Downers Grover, IL: InterVarsity Press, 2010), 115.

5. See Robert Webber, *The Younger Evangelicals: Facing the Challenges of the New World* (Grand Rapids, MI: Baker Books, 2002).

6. See http://www.opendoortoday.org.

7. See http://villageanglican.church/whoweare/.

8. "Voices on Church Planting," Fuller Studio, https://fullerstudio .fuller.edu/church-planting/.

9. To find out more about Resurrection Anglican Church South Austin, visit http:// www.rezaustin.com.

10. Thomas Merton, *New Seeds of Contemplation* (New York: New Direction Books, 1961), 31.

Chapter 10: Bringing Liturgy Home

1. See https://lectionary.library.vanderbilt.edu.

2. Renzo Bonetti, *Signs of Love: Christian Liturgy in the Everyday Life of the Family* (Franklin, TN: Seedbed Publishing, 2012), 4.

3. Thomas Grady and Paula Huston, eds., *Signatures of Grace: Catholic Writers on the Sacraments* (Eugene, OR: Wipf & Stock Publishers, 2001), 220.

Epilogue

1. Quoted in Esther de Wall, *Seeking Life: The Baptismal Invitation of the Rule of St. Benedict* (Collegeville, MN: Liturgical Press, 2009), 26.

2. Leonard Sweet, *Soul Tsunami: Sink or Swim in the New Millennium Culture* (Grand Rapids, MI: Zondervan, 1999), 17.

3. Brian Zahnd, "A Premodern Sacramental Eclectic," Personal Blog, June 24, 2013, https://brianzahnd.com/2013/06/a-pre modern-sacramental-eclectic/.